Air Pollution : Causes and Control

Air Pollution : Causes and Control

Yashpal Wadhwa

CYBER TECH PUBLICATIONS
4264/3, Ansari Road, Daryaganj, New Delhi-110002 (India)
Ph.: 011-23244078. Fax: 011-23280028
E-Mail: cyberpublicationsdelhi@yahoo.com

AIR POLLUTION : CAUSES AND CONTROL

Yashpal Wadhwa

First Edition 2009

Published by :

G.S. Rawat for **Cyber Tech Publications**
4264/3, Ansari Road, Daryaganj, New Delhi-110002 (India)
Ph.: 011-23244078. Fax: 011-23280028
E-Mail: cyberpublicationsdelhi@yahoo.com

Printed at :

Preface

In recent years our environment has been dealt with on a very serious level. Today's generation has demanded that something be done to preserve our environment. They are speaking out and asking countless questions. In many ways the environment has been damaged beyond repair. The focus today is on repairing and preserving what remains. The physical aspects of air pollution and its effects on society is the theme of this unit. A teacher would be free to approach the topic from several directions. For example, one could discuss each pollutant individually in terms of sources, methods of emission, how it is affected by chemical reactions in the atmosphere, adverse effects, and ultimate fate, Others may prefer to emphasize the functional approach because in most regions where air pollution is considered a problem, a pollutant coexists with other pollutants and there is a continual evolution of the nature of the atmosphere through chemical reactions.

This book deals in all the spheres of Pollution its causes and control methods. Undersigned has done tireless efforts for bringing out this book and is confident enough that this work of him would be beneficial and informative to the teachers, students and general readers alike. Suggestions and complaints are always welcome.

—Author

CONTENTS

1

Introduction: Air Pollution

The term "air pollution" is used to describe substances that are artificially introduced into the air. Air pollution stems from gases and airborne particles which, in excess, are harmful to human health, buildings and ecosystems.

Four major impacts determine the classification of pollutants under the traditional policy field Air Pollution :

- The acidification of soil and water by pollutants such as sulphur oxides, nitrogen oxides and ammonia;
- The damage to buildings sensitive to the same acidifying substances;
- The formation of tropospheric ozone from so-called ozone precursors, e.g. volatile organic compounds, nitrogen oxides and carbon monoxide which indirectly affect human and animal health and vegetation;
- Direct effects on human health and ecosystems e.g. through high atmospheric concentrations of particles, and VOCs.

Excluded from this chapter are emissions of CO_2, N_2O, CH 4 and CFCs, which are covered in the policy fields Climate Change and Ozone Layer Depletion. Emissions of highly toxic substances are given special consideration under the heading Dispersion of Toxic Substances.

Although some of these pollutants are also produced by nature, the main environmental problems result from human activities. Air pollutants are often transported over considerable distances, affecting air quality, ecosystems, lakes and other surface water, groundwater, soils and buildings in adjacent and distant countries.

The Fifth Environmental Action Programme (5EAP) treats Air Pollution under Section 5.2: "Acidification and air quality." Public concern is focused mainly on damage to forests and smog, though in Nordic countries emphasis is also placed on the acidification of lakes. The main EU air directives cover emissions of SO_2 (AP-3) and NO x (AP-1) from large combustion plants, the sulphur contents of fossil fuels (AP-6), and emission limits for transport vehicles (AP-5).

Many of these specific measures have been underpinned by the UNECE Convention on Long-Range Transboundary Air Pollution, which was adopted in 1979 and signed by 35 countries, including EU Member States.

The 5EAP lists the following targets to reduce air pollution:

- SO_2 emissions : reduction by 35% from 1985 levels by 2000,
- NOx emissions : reduction by 30% from 1980 levels by 2000,
- VOC emissions : reduction by 30% from 1990 levels by 1999.

The following list of indicators selected by the Scientific Advisory Group (SAG) "Air Pollution" comprises four indicators of pressure. The two "background" or "driving force" indicators Consumption of petrol & diesel oil by road vehicles and Primary energy consumption represent the major causes of these pressures.

AIR POLLUTION

Air pollution is the modification of the natural characteristics of the atmosphere by a chemical, particulate matter, or biological agent. The atmosphere is a complex, dynamic natural gaseous system that is essential to support life on planet Earth. Stratospheric ozone depletion due to air pollution has long been recognized as a threat to human health as well as to the Earth's ecosystems.

Worldwide air pollution is responsible for large numbers of deaths and cases of respiratory disease. While major stationary sources are often identified with air pollution, the greatest source of emissions is actually mobile sources, mainly automobiles. Gases such as carbon dioxide, which contribute to global warming, have recently gained recognition as pollutants by climate scientists, while they also recognize that carbon dioxide is essential for plant life through photosynthesis.

Pollutants

There are many substances in the air which may impair the health of plants and animals (including humans), or reduce visibility. These arise both from natural processes and human activity. Substances not naturally found in the air or at greater concentrations or in different locations from usual are referred to as pollutants.

Pollutants can be classified as either primary or secondary. Primary pollutants are substances directly emitted from a process, such as ash from a volcanic eruption or the carbon monoxide gas from a motor vehicle exhaust.

Secondary pollutants are not emitted directly. Rather, they form in the air when primary pollutants react or interact. An important example of a secondary pollutant is ground level ozone-one of the many secondary pollutants that make up photochemical smog.

Note that some pollutants may be both primary and secondary: that is, they are both emitted directly and formed from other primary pollutants.

Major primary pollutants produced by human activity include:

- Sulfur oxides (SOx) especially sulfur dioxide are emitted from burning of coal and oil.
- Nitrogen oxides (NOx) especially nitrogen dioxide are emitted from high temperature combustion. Can be seen as the brown haze dome above or plume downwind of cities.
- Carbon monoxide is colourless, odourless, non-irritating but very poisonous gas. It is a product by incomplete combustion of fuel such as natural gas, coal or wood. Vehicular exhaust is a major source of carbon monoxide.
- Carbon dioxide (CO_2), a greenhouse gas emitted from combustion.
- Volatile organic compounds (VOC), such as hydrocarbon fuel vapors and solvents.
- Particulate matter (PM), measured as smoke and dust. PM10 is the fraction of suspended particles 10 micrometers in diameter and smaller that will enter the nasal cavity. PM2.5 has a maximum particle size of 2.5 μm and will enter the bronchies and lungs.
- Toxic metals, such as lead, cadmium and copper.
- Chlorofluorocarbons (CFCs), harmful to the ozone layer emitted from products currently banned from use.
- Ammonia (NH3) emitted from agricultural processes.
- Odors, such as from garbage, sewage, and industrial processes

- Radioactive pollutants produced by nuclear explosions and war explosives, and natural processes such as radon.

Secondary pollutants include:

- Particulate matter formed from gaseous primary pollutants and compounds in photochemical smog, such as nitrogen dioxide.
- Ground level ozone (O_3) formed from NOx and VOCs.
- Peroxyacetyl nitrate (PAN) similarly formed from NOx and VOCs.

Minor air pollutants include:

- A large number of minor hazardous air pollutants. Some of these are regulated in USA under the Clean Air Act and in Europe under the Air Framework Directive.
- A variety of persistent organic pollutants, which can attach to particulate matter.

Sources of Air Pollution

Sources of air pollution refer to the various locations, activities or factors which are responsible for the releasing of pollutants in the atmosphere. These sources can be classified into two major categories which are:

Anthropogenic sources (human activity) mostly related to burning different kinds of fuel:

- "Stationary Sources" as smoke stacks of power plants, manufacturing facilities, municipal waste incinerators.
- "Mobile Sources" as motor vehicles, aircraft etc.
- Marine vessels, such as container ships or cruise ships, and related port air pollution.
- Burning wood, fireplaces, stoves, furnaces and incinerators.

- Oil refining, and industrial activity in general.
- Chemicals, dust and controlled burn practices in agriculture and forestry management, (see Dust Bowl).
- Fumes from paint, hair spray, varnish, aerosol sprays and other solvents.
- Waste deposition in landfills, which generate methane.
- Military, such as nuclear weapons, toxic gases, germ warfare and rocketry.

Natural Sources

- Dust from natural sources, usually large areas of land with little or no vegetation.
- Methane, emitted by the digestion of food by animals, for example cattle.
- Radon gas from radioactive decay within the Earth's crust.
- Smoke and carbon monoxide from wildfires.
- Volcanic activity, which produce sulfur, chlorine, and ash particulates.

Air Pollutant Emission Factors

Air pollutant emission factors are representative values that attempt to relate the quantity of a pollutant released to the ambient air with an activity associated with the release of that pollutant. These factors are usually expressed as the weight of pollutant divided by a unit weight, volume, distance, or duration of the activity emitting the pollutant (e.g., kilograms of particulate emitted per megagram of coal burned). Such factors facilitate estimation of emissions from various sources of air pollution. In most cases, these factors are simply averages of all available data of acceptable quality, and are generally assumed to be representative of long-term averages.

The United States Environmental Protection Agency has published a compilation of air pollutant emission factors for a multitude of industrial sources. The United Kingdom, Australia, Canada and other countries have published similar compilations, as has the European Environment Agency.

INDOOR AIR QUALITY (IAQ)

A lack of ventilation indoors concentrates air pollution where people often spend the majority of their time. Radon (Rn) gas, a carcinogen, is exuded from the Earth in certain locations and trapped inside houses. Building materials including carpeting and plywood emit formaldehyde (H_2CO) gas. Paint and solvents give off volatile organic compounds (VOCs) as they dry.

Lead paint can degenerate into dust and be inhaled. Intentional air pollution is introduced with the use of air fresheners, incense, and other scented items. Controlled wood fires in stoves and fireplaces can add significant amounts of smoke particulates into the air, inside and out. Indoor pollution fatalities may be caused by using pesticides and other chemical sprays indoors without proper ventilation.

Carbon monoxide (CO) poisoning and fatalities are often caused by faulty vents and chimneys, or by the burning of charcoal indoors. Chronic carbon monoxide poisoning can result even from poorly adjusted pilot lights. Traps are built into all domestic plumbing to keep sewer gas, hydrogen sulfide, out of interiors. Clothing emits tetrachloroethylene, or other dry cleaning fluids, for days after dry cleaning.

Though its use has now been banned in many countries, the extensive use of asbestos in industrial and domestic environments in the past has left a potentially very dangerous material in many localities. Asbestosis is a chronic inflammatory medical condition affecting the tissue of the lungs. It occurs after long-term, heavy exposure to asbestos from asbestos-containing materials in structures. Sufferers have severe dyspnea (shortness of breath) and are at an increased risk regarding several different types of lung cancer.

As clear explanations are not always stressed in non-technical literature, care should be taken to distinguish between several forms of relevant diseases. According to the World Health Organisation (WHO), these may defined as; asbestosis, lung cancer, and mesothelioma (generally a very rare form of cancer, when more widespread it is almost always associated with prolonged exposure to asbestos).

Biological sources of air pollution are also found indoors, as gases and airborne particulates. Pets produce dander, people produce dust from minute skin flakes and decomposed hair, dust mites in bedding, carpeting and furniture produce enzymes and micron-sized fecal droppings, inhabitants emit methane, mold forms in walls and generates mycotoxins and spores, air conditioning systems can incubate Legionnaires' disease and mold, and houseplants, soil and surrounding gardens can produce pollen, dust, and mold.

Indoors, the lack of air circulation allows these airborne pollutants to accumulate more than they would otherwise occur in nature.

Health Effects

The World Health Organization states that 2.4 million people die each year from causes directly attributable to air pollution. Many of these mortalities are attributable to indoor air pollution. Worldwide more deaths per year are linked to air pollution than to automobile accidents. Published in 2005 suggests that 310,000 Europeans die from air pollution annually. Direct causes of air pollution related deaths include aggravated asthma, bronchitis, emphysema, lung and heart diseases, and respiratory allergies. The US EPA estimates that a proposed set of changes in diesel engine technology (Tier 2) could result in 12,000 fewer premature mortalities, 15,000 fewer heart attacks, 6,000 fewer emergency room visits by children with asthma, and 8,900 fewer respiratory-related hospital admissions each year in the United States.

The worst short term civilian pollution crisis in India was the 1984 Bhopal Disaster. Leaked industrial vapors from the Union Carbide factory, belonging to Union Carbide, Inc., U.S.A., killed more than 2,000 people outright and injured anywhere from 150,000 to 600,000 others, some 6,000 of whom would later die from their injuries.

The United Kingdom suffered its worst air pollution event when the December 4th Great Smog of 1952 formed over London. In six days more than 4,000 died, and 8,000 more died within the following months.

An accidental leak of anthrax spores from a biological warfare laboratory in the former USSR in 1979 near Sverdlovsk is believed to have been the cause of hundreds of civilian deaths. The worst single incident of air pollution to occur in the United States of America occurred in Donora, Pennsylvania in late October, 1948, when 20 people died and over 7,000 were injured.

The health effects caused by air pollutants may range from subtle biochemical and physiological changes to difficulty in breathing, wheezing, coughing and aggravation of existing respiratory and cardiac conditions.

These effects can result in increased medication use, increased doctor or emergency room visits, more hospital admissions and premature death. The human health effects of poor air quality are far reaching, but principally affect the body's respiratory system and the cardiovascular system. Individual reactions to air pollutants depend on the type of pollutant a person is exposed to, the degree of exposure, the individual's health status and genetics.

Reduction Efforts

There are various air pollution control technologies and urban planning strategies available to reduce air pollution.

Efforts to reduce pollution from mobile sources includes primary regulation (many developing countries have permissive regulations), expanding regulation to new sources (such as cruise and transport ships, farm equipment, and small gas-powered equipment such as lawn trimmers, chainsaws, and snowmobiles), increased fuel efficiency (such as through the use of hybrid vehicles), conversion to cleaner fuels (such as bioethanol, biodiesel, or conversion to electric vehicles).

Control Devices

The following items are commonly used as pollution control devices by industry or transportation devices. They can either destroy contaminants or remove them from an exhaust stream before it is emitted into the atmosphere.

AIR POLLUTION CAUSES AND EFFECTS

History

Humans probably first experienced harm from air pollution when they built fires in poorly ventilated caves. Since then we have gone on to pollute more of the earth's surface. Until recently, environmental pollution problems have been local and minor because of the Earth's own ability to absorb and purify minor quantities of pollutants. The industrialization of society, the introduction of motorized vehicles, and the explosion of the population, are factors contributing toward the growing air pollution problem. At this time it is urgent that we find methods to clean up the air.

The primary air pollutants found in most urban areas are carbon monoxide, nitrogen oxides, sulfur oxides, hydrocarbons, and particulate matter (both solid and liquid). These pollutants are dispersed throughout the world's atmosphere in concentrations high enough to gradually cause serious health problems. Serious health problems can occur quickly when air pollutants are concentrated, such as when massive injections of sulfur dioxide and suspended particulate matter are emitted by a large volcanic eruption.

Air Pollution in the Home

You cannot escape air pollution, not even in your own home. "In 1985 the Environmental Protection Agency (EPA) reported that toxic chemicals found in the air of almost every American home are three times more likely to cause some type of cancer than outdoor air pollutants". The health problems in these buildings are called "sick building syndrome". "An estimated one-fifth to one-third of all U.S. buildings are now considered "sick".

The EPA has found that the air in some office buildings is 100 times more polluted than the air outside. Poor ventilation causes about half of the indoor air pollution problems. The rest come from specific sources such as copying machines, electrical and telephone cables, mold and microbe-harboring air conditioning systems and ducts, cleaning fluids, cigarette smoke, carpet, latex caulk and paint, vinyl molding, linoleum tile, and building materials and furniture that emit air pollutants such as formaldehyde.

A major indoor air pollutant is radon-222, a colorless, odorless, tasteless, naturally occurring radioactive gas produced by the radioactive decay of uranium-238. "According to studies by the EPA and the National Research Council, exposure to radon is second only to smoking as a cause of lung cancer". Radon enters through pores and cracks in concrete when indoor air pressure is less than the pressure of gasses in the soil. Indoor air will be healthier than outdoor air if you use an energy recovery ventilator to provide a consistent supply of fresh filtered air and then seal air leaks in the shell of your home.

Sources of Pollutants

The two main sources of pollutants in urban areas are transportation (predominantly automobiles) and fuel combustion in stationary sources, including residential, commercial, and industrial heating and cooling and coal-burning power plants. Motor vehicles produce high levels of carbon monoxides (CO) and a major source of hydrocarbons (HC) and nitrogen oxides (NOx). Whereas, fuel combustion in stationary sources is the dominant source of sulfur dioxide (SO_2).

Carbon Dioxide

Carbon dioxide (CO_2) is one of the major pollutants in the atmosphere. Major sources of CO_2 are fossil fuels burning and deforestation. "The concentrations of CO_2 in the air around 1860 before the effects of industrialization were felt, is assumed to have been about 290 parts per million (ppm). In the hundred years and more since then, the concentration has increased by about 30 to 35 ppm that is by 10 percent". Industrial countries account for 65% of CO_2 emissions with the United States and Soviet Union responsible for 50%. Less developed countries (LDCs), with 80% of the world's people, are responsible for 35% of CO_2 emissions but may contribute 50% by 2020. "Carbon dioxide emissions are increasing by 4% a year".

In 1975, 18 thousand million tons of carbon dioxide (equivalent to 5 thousand million tons of carbon) were released into the atmosphere, but the atmosphere showed an increase of only 8 billion tons (equivalent to 2.2 billion tons of carbon". The ocean waters contain about sixty times more CO_2 than the atmosphere. If the equilibrium is disturbed by externally increasing the concentration of CO_2 in the air, then the oceans would absorb more and more CO_2. If the oceans can no longer keep pace, then more CO_2 will remain into the atmosphere. As water warms, its ability to absorb CO_2 is reduced.

CO_2 is a good transmitter of sunlight, but partially restricts infrared radiation going back from the earth into space. This produces the so-called greenhouse effect that prevents a drastic cooling of the Earth during the night.

Increasing the amount of CO_2 in the atmosphere reinforces this effect and is expected to result in a warming of the Earth's surface. Currently carbon dioxide is responsible for 57% of the global warming trend. Nitrogen oxides contribute most of the atmospheric contaminants.

N0X-nitric oxide (N0) and nitrogen dioxide ($N0_2$):

- Natural component of the Earth's atmosphere.
- Important in the formation of both acid precipitation and photochemical smog (ozone), and causes nitrogen loading.
- Comes from the burning of biomass and fossil fuels.
- 30 to 50 million tons per year from human activities, and natural 10 to 20 million tons per year.
- Average residence time in the atmosphere is days.
- Has a role in reducing stratospheric ozone.

N20-nitrous oxide:

- Natural component of the Earth's atmosphere.
- Important in the greenhouse effect and causes nitrogen loading.
- Human inputs 6 million tons per year, and 19 million tons per year by nature.
- Residence time in the atmosphere about 170 years

- 1700 (285 parts per billion), 1990 (310 parts per billion), 2030 (340 parts per billion).
- Comes from nitrogen based fertilizers, deforestation, and biomass burning.

Sulfur and Chlorofluorocarbons (CFCs)

Sulfur dioxide is produced by combustion of sulfur-containing fuels, such as coal and fuel oils. Also, in the process of producing sulfuric acid and in metallurgical process involving ores that contain sulfur.

Sulfur oxides can injure man, plants and materials. At sufficiently high concentrations, sulfur dioxide irritates the upper respiratory tract of human beings because potential effect of sulfur dioxide is to make breathing more difficult by causing the finer air tubes of the lung to constrict. "Power plants and factories emit 90% to 95% of the sulfur dioxide and 57% of the nitrogen oxides in the United States. Almost 60% of the SO_2 emissions are released by tall smoke stakes, enabling the emissions to travel long distances".

As emissions of sulfur dioxide and nitric oxide from stationary sources are transported long distances by winds, they form secondary pollutants such as nitrogen dioxide, nitric acid vapor, and droplets containing solutions of sulfuric acid, sulfate, and nitrate salts. These chemicals descend to the earth's surface in wet form as rain or snow and in dry form as a gases fog, dew, or solid particles. This is known as acid deposition or acid rain.

Chlorofluorocarbons (CFCs)

CFCs are lowering the average concentration of ozone in the stratosphere. "Since 1978 the use of CFCs in aerosol cans has been banned in the United States, Canada, and most Scandinavian countries. Aerosols are still the largest use, accounting for 25% of global CFC use". Spray cans, discarded or leaking refrigeration and air conditioning equipment, and the burning plastic foam products release the CFCs into the atmosphere. Depending on the type, CFCs stay in the atmosphere from 22 to 111 years. Chlorofluorocarbons move up to the stratosphere gradually over several decades. Under high energy ultra violet (UV) radiation, they break down and release chlorine atoms, which speed up the breakdown of ozone (O_3) into oxygen gas (O_2).

Chlorofluorocarbons, also known as Freons, are greenhouse gases that contribute to global warming. Photochemical air pollution is commonly referred to as "smog". Smog, a contraction of the words smoke and fog, has been caused throughout recorded history by water condensing on smoke particles, usually from burning coal. With the introduction of petroleum to replace coal economies in countries, photochemical smog has become predominant in many cities, which are located in sunny, warm, and dry climates with many motor vehicles. The worst episodes of photochemical smog tend to occur in summer.

Smog

Photochemical smog is also appearing in regions of the tropics and subtropics where savanna grasses are periodically burned. Smog's unpleasant properties result from the irradiation by sunlight of hydrocarbons caused primarily by unburned gasoline emitted by automobiles and other combustion sources. The products of photochemical reactions includes organic particles, ozone, aldehydes, ketones, peroxyacetyl nitrate, organic acids, and other oxidants. Ozone is a gas created by nitrogen dioxide or nitric oxide when exposed to sunlight. Ozone causes eye irritation, impaired lung function, and damage to trees and crops. Another form of smog is called industrial smog.

This smog is created by burning coal and heavy oil that contain sulfur impurities in power plants, industrial plants, etc... The smog consists mostly of a mixture of sulfur dioxide and fog. Suspended droplets of sulfuric acid are formed from some of the sulfur dioxide, and a variety of suspended solid particles. This smog is common during the winter in cities such as London, Chicago, Pittsburgh. When these cities burned large amounts of coal and heavy oil without control of the output, large-scale problems were witnessed. In 1952 London, England, 4,000 people died as a result of this form of fog. Today coal and heavy oil are burned only in large boilers and with reasonably good control or tall smokestacks so that industrial smog is less of a problem. However, some countries such as China, Poland, Czechoslovakia, and some other eastern European countries, still burn large quantities of coal without using adequate controls.

Pollution Damage to Plants

With the destruction and burning of the rain forests more and more CO_2 is being released into the atmosphere. Trees play an important role in producing oxygen from carbon dioxide. "A 115 year old Beech tree exposes about 200,000 leaves with a total surface to 1200 square meters. During the course of one sunny day such a tree inhales 9,400 liters of carbon dioxide to produce 12 kilograms of carbohydrate, thus liberating 9,400 liters of oxygen. Through this mechanism about 45,000 liters of air are regenerated which is sufficient for the respiration of 2 to 3 people". This process is called photosynthesis which all plants go though but some yield more and some less oxygen. As long as no more wood is burnt than is reproduced by the forests, no change in atmospheric CO_2 concentration will result.

Pollutants such as sulfur dioxide, nitrogen oxides, ozone and peroxyacl nitrates (PANs), cause direct damage to leaves of crop plants and trees when they enter leaf pores (stomates). Chronic exposure of leaves and needles to air pollutants can also break down the waxy coating that helps prevent excessive water loss and damage from diseases, pests, drought and frost. "In the midwestern United States crop losses of wheat, corn, soybeans, and peanuts from damage by ozone and acid deposition amount to about $5 billion a year".

Reducing Pollution

You can help to reduce global air pollution and climate change by driving a car that gets at least 35 miles a gallon, walking, bicycling, and using mass transit when possible. Replace incandescent light bulbs with compact fluorescent bulbs, make your home more energy efficient, and buy only energy efficient appliances. Recycle newspapers, aluminum, and other materials.

Plant trees and avoid purchasing products such as Styrofoam that contain CFCs. Support much stricter clean air laws and enforcement of international treaties to reduce ozone depletion and slow global warming.

Earth is everybody's home and nobody likes living in a dirty home. Together, we can make the earth a cleaner, healthier and more pleasant place to live.

CLIMATE CHANGE

The Earths atmosphere keeps the planet warm. Without the warming cover of natural greenhouse gases, mainly carbon dioxide (CO_2) and water vapour, life could not exist on Earth. Through the release of greenhouse gases such as CO_2, methane, CFCs and N_2O caused by human activities, our climate will change. How fast, and where exactly, is still controversial, but there is consensus in the scientific community that the consequences may be serious:

- The expected rise in sea levels may threaten islands and nations with low coast lines;
- Changes in rainfall levels and patterns may affect natural vegetation, agriculture and forestry;

- The loss of biodiversity may be accelerated if climate zones move so fast that species (e.g. in rain forests) cannot follow them;
- Weather anomalies such as hurricanes may occur more frequently, causing immense damage to humans and their property, and to nature.

Not all possible consequences are fully understood. For example, it is very uncertain:

- To what extent greenhouse gas-induced disturbances of the ocean-atmosphere equilibrium contribute to altered global circulation patterns such as the El Niño phenomenon;
- Whether the gulf stream, Europes central heating, could change its direction and/or intensity, thus leading to a drastic cooling of Europes climate;

The Member States of the European Union are responsible for about one quarter of the global anthropogenic greenhouse gas emissions. A global strategy must also take into account the emissions caused by rapid economic growth in developing countries.

Most of these nations are technology buyers using, voluntarily or forced by the markets, energy-relevant technologies such as cars and power plants that are developed and produced in Europe, Japan and the USA. Progress towards more energy-efficient technologies in the EU may therefore have strong positive side-effects in other regions of the globe that may even be greater, in the long run, than the direct emission reductions observed in the EU itself.

At the 1992 United Nations Conference on Environment and Development held in Rio de Janeiro, the Framework Convention on Climate Change was adopted as the basis for global political action. Under this convention, new commitments to reduce emissions of greenhouse gases beyond the year 2000 were agreed in Kyoto in December 1997. The Kyoto Protocol, adopted by consensus by some 150 parties, stipulates that Annex 1 Parties (mainly industrialised countries) shall individually or jointly reduce their aggregate emissions of a "basket" of six greenhouse gases to 5% below 1990 levels in the period 2008-2012.

In contrast to this political target, the scientific community speaking through the voice of the Intergovernmental Panel on Climate Change (IPCC) demands a much more substantial three-quarter reduction of the current greenhouse gas emissions. This would require an almost complete phasing out of fossil fuels, with significant (but overall not necessarily negative) consequences for Europes economies.

For its part the EU undertook to reduce by 8% over the next 15 years emissions that cause global warming, compared with 7% for USA and 6% for Japan and Canada. The reduction target is calculated using the Greenhouse Warming Potentials (GWP) developed by the IPCC as "weighting coefficients", and thus is perhaps a first example how a future "Pressure Index Climate Change" could be used to monitor the implementation of the Kyoto process on the basis of one simple statistical figure.

The following indicators show how far the European Union has been successful in reducing greenhouse gas emissions. NOx and SO_2, although not greenhouse gases, have been added following the recommendations of the Scientific Advisory Groups (SAG) on Climate Change, because they play an important role in the scientific interpretation of global temperature trends.

Loss of Biodiversity

The Global Convention on Biological Diversity, signed in 1992 at the Earth Summit, describes biodiversity as the "variability among all living organisms from all sources, including terrestrial, marine and other aquatic ecosystems and ecological complexes of which they are part, this includes diversity within species, between species and of ecosystems."

Among the ten policy fields, Loss of Biodiversity is probably the most controversial one. The diversity of nature is the result of an evolutionary process that started about two billion years ago. When looking, for example, at the destruction of rain forests over the last twenty years, it becomes obvious that mankind is destroying this heritage at an incredible speed. Not surprisingly, the biodiversity debate is laden with ethical, sometimes religious arguments. It was probably a biologist who has coined the saying "dont put price tags on my butterflies" ; however, economic reality puts "price tags" on biodiversity every day, mostly ignoring the moral considerations raised by experts.

The number of species endangered by human activities and the number of natural or semi-natural habitats being destroyed, fragmented or changed are constantly growing, thus destabilising ecosystems, causing the loss of vital resources together with genetic and cultural impoverishment.

Europe covers only 7% of the Earths land surface but contains a large biodiversity due to natural fragmentation by rivers, mountains, seas, the influences of glaciation, etc. The pressures on European biodiversity emanate from all sectors of society, with agriculture, forestry and transport being particularly responsible for habitat loss and fragmentation.

Measuring pressure on biodiversity, although an ambitious task, is essential to supply the controversial biodiversity debate with (hopefully) non-controversial, neutral and objective figures. Given the complexity of the issue, one should not expect perfect solutions. Describing threats to the "health" of ecosystems with just six indicators will resemble very much what a doctor would advise a human patient:

"stop smoking, drink less, avoid fat meals and ride your bicycle every day." Most of the following indicators are of this rather general character. They are no substitute for a proper diagnosis, or a detailed plan to preserve a valuable habitat, but they may serve to publicly monitor the biggest threats to European biodiversity.

Please note that this chapter focuses on pressures on terrestrial biodiversity. The biodiversity of marine ecosystems is treated within the separate policy field Marine Environment & Coastal Zones. Forest ecosystem matters will be included in the biodiversity chapter, whereas economic aspects such as wood consumption will be treated under Resource Depletion.

2

Air Pollutants-their Sources and Effects

CARBON MONOXIDE

Carbon monoxide (CO) is a colourless, odourless and tasteless gas. Major sources include motor vehicles, home heating systems, and refuse burning. Outdoors, CO is generally a problem pollutant only in congested urban centres with high traffic density, especially in winter, as vehicle engines produce more pollution in cold weather.

In some traffic conditions, drivers and passengers in vehicles may be exposed to higher levels of CO than pedestrians in city streets. Malfunctioning or badly-vented heating furnaces, gas cooking stoves or woodstoves may also produce dangerous levels of CO in buildings. Other environments with an above-average risk of elevated CO levels include ice skating rinks, parking garages and traffic tunnels (WHO, 1999).

Background concentrations of CO in remote parts of the Northern hemisphere are around 0.1 ppm (WHO, 1999). Average annual concentrations in centres across Canada range from 0.5 to 1.0 ppm (Environment Canada, 2002). If inhaled, CO quickly enters the blood stream, where it reduces the ability of the blood to deliver oxygen to the organs and tissues of the body. The health impact of CO is most serious for those who suffer from cardiovascular disease, although healthy individuals are also affected at higher concentrations. Exposure to elevated levels is associated with numerous symptoms, including headache, fatigue, confusion, nausea, and impairment of vision. Work capacity, learning ability and the ability to perform complex tasks are reduced.

Nitrogen Dioxide

Nitrogen dioxide (NO Sulphur dioxide (SO_2) is a colourless gas with a characteristic smell, like that of a struck match. When levels reach between 0.3 to 1.0 parts per million (ppm), it is generally detectable as an acidic taste in the air. SO_2 dissolves very readily in water, eventually forming sulphuric acid. SO_2 is one of the most significant pollutants in many industrialised nations: it is often emitted as a result of burning sulphur-containing fuels, and by metal smelters and oil refineries.

Emissions of SO_2 from motor vehicles are relatively minor. Health effects associated with exposure to high concentrations of sulphur dioxide include breathing discomfort, respiratory illness, alterations in the lungs' normal defences, and aggravation of existing respiratory and cardiovascular disease. People with asthma, chronic lung or heart disease are the most sensitive to SO_2.

Apart from effects on human health, SO_2 can also directly damage the leaves of trees, and agricultural crops. SO_2 also has important indirect impacts by contributing to acid rain, which acidifies lakes and rivers, speeds up the corrosion of masonry and metal objects, and removes essential elements from the soil.

Sulphur dioxide also contributes to the formation of acid aerosols (fine acidic particles), which may have detrimental health effects. These small particles cause a visual haze, which affects the enjoyment of scenic vistas and has an effect on the earth's radiation balance.

Hydrogen Sulphide

Hydrogen sulphide (H_2S) is a colourless gas with a characteristic smell of rotten eggs. H_2S is flammable and can form an explosive mixture with air or oxygen. Common sources of H^2S include pulp and paper mills, oil refineries, steel processing plants, natural gas plants, and sewage treatment systems. Natural sources include sulphurous hot springs and volcanic vents, swamps and bogs. Naturally-occurring sulphate-reducing bacteria can also produce H^2S in domestic water systems. The processes which produce hydrogen sulphide often generate other sulphur-containing compounds, such as methyl mercaptan and dimethylsulphide. These substances are also highly malodorous, and are often grouped together with hydrogen sulphide and referred to as total reduced sulphur compounds, or TRS. In the ambient air, the undesirable effects of H_2S are generally felt in terms of a bad odour. The odour threshold for H_2S is generally 1-5 ppb, but can be lower for some individuals. Background concentrations in unpolluted areas are around 0.1 ppb (WHO, 2003). There is some evidence that persistent exposure to unpleasant odours may have a significant effect on community health: review and monitoring of relevant health studies continues. There is also evidence that H_2S can contribute to an increased rate of spontaneous abortions when annual concentrations exceed approximately 3 ppb.

At higher concentrations (from 2 to approximately 100 ppm) hydrogen sulphide affects the mucous membranes, causing eye and throat irritation. Above this level H_2S becomes life-threatening as the sense of smell is impaired, removing the body's normal warning signal.

High concentrations of hydrogen sulphide can also cause paint discoloration and metal corrosion, and are damaging to plants. Life-threatening levels, in excess of 300 ppm, can exist in underground sewer pipe systems and occasionally above ground near sewer manholes, in situations where sewer gases are released from underground piping. During drilling for oil and gas, blow-outs can also occur with the release of large quantities of H_2S. Ambient concentrations in New Brunswick, even in the vicinity of large emission sources, seldom exceed 40 ppb (0.04 ppm).

Total Reduced Sulphur

Total Reduced Sulphur (TRS) is a family of odorous compounds including hydrogen sulphide, methyl sulphide, dimethyl sulphide and dimethyl disulphide. Some common sources of TRS include petroleum refineries, storage tanks for unrefined petroleum products, natural gas plants, petrochemical plants, sewage treatment facilities, and pulp and paper plants that use the kraft pulping process. Monitoring in the vicinity of kraft pulp mills in New Brunswick generally includes TRS. When evaluating monitoring data for TRS, reference may be made to standards or objectives for hydrogen sulphide. Although hydrogen sulphide may be a major component of TRS, the exact proportion is not known unless specific analysis for both H_2S and TRS is performed.

Ground-Level Ozone

Ozone (O_3) is a reactive, unstable form of oxygen. In very high concentrations, it is a bluish gas. The characteristic sharp smell of ozone may be recognised around electrical equipment such as motors or arc welders, where it is formed by the high temperature electric spark. In the concentrations found in outdoor air, even in the most severe pollution episodes, ozone is both colourless and odourless. Ozone is not emitted directly from smokestacks and exhaust pipes, but is formed in the air from other pollutants, most importantly nitrogen oxides (NO_2) and hydrocarbons or VOCs (such as solvent and gasoline vapours).

Vehicle exhaust contains all the necessary compounds to produce ozone, and, as a result, cars and trucks are important contributors to ground level ozone concentrations. Industrial emissions of NOx and hydrocarbons are also significant precursor emissions for ground level ozone.

Slow-moving air and strong sunshine greatly speed up the formation of ozone. As a result, ground level ozone is not typically a problem pollutant in the cooler months, but is likely to be more significant in hot, hazy summer weather. Such haze may build up over a period of days into a "photochemical smog".

However, the yellow or brownish colour of such smog is usually due to nitrogen dioxide and fine chemical particles, not the ground level ozone itself. Because the formation of ground level ozone depends on weather conditions, the severity of ozone pollution can be very variable from one year to the next.

In New Brunswick, significant ozone episodes occur on average about six times per summer, mainly affecting the southern part of the province. Much of this ozone originates from populated regions of the north-eastern United States, especially the Washington to Boston "corridor".

Ground-level ozone irritates the lungs, causing airway inflammation, and can make breathing difficult. Exposure to high concentrations can result in chest tightness, shortness of breath, reduced lung capacity and exercise performance, and coughing and wheezing. Recent health research suggests there is no clear "safe" threshold for ozone. Asthmatics appear to be more sensitive to repeat ozone exposures than healthy subjects. Concentrations as low as 60 ppb cause a measurable reduction in exercise performance.

There appears to be an additive or synergistic effect between ozone and some other principal air pollutants such as SO^2 and NO^2 (Health Canada, 1999). Ground level ozone can cause damage to agricultural crops which are ozone-sensitive, such as potatoes and tomatoes. It can also cause noticeable leaf damage in other species. Forest trees and other vegetation may be injured, or growth inhibited. Ozone also weakens rubber, and attacks metals and painted surfaces (Bates, 1980; Multistakeholder NOx/VOC Science Program, 1997c).

Ozone levels are often lower in city centres than in surrounding rural areas. This is because ozone reacts with nitrogen oxides, often found in relatively high concentrations in city cores due to emissions from motor vehicles. This effect is seen in Saint John, although to a lesser extent than in larger cities.

Total Suspended Particulate (TSP) Particles in the air (also called "particulates" by air pollution scientists) may either be of natural origin or the result of human activity. Some common natural sources and types of particulates include wind-blown soil dust, forest fires, sea salt, volcanoes, and plants (which produce pollen and spores). Human activities which generate particles include fuel combustion (domestic and industrial) and any other burning (e.g.waste incineration or slash burning); travel on dirt roads, construction work, and mining and quarrying. Dust on road and work sites is often wetted down to control particulate emissions. Other kinds of particles form in the air when gases such as sulphur dioxide (SO_2) and nitrogen oxides(NOx) react together. These particles are partly responsible for the yellowish "smog" sometimes seen over large cities.

"Total suspended particulate" (TSP) hasbeen a standard pollution measurement for many years, obtained by drawing a large volume of air through a special filter.This method makes no distinction between natural particles, such as pollen and spores, and particles which are emitted from vehicles or smokestacks.

People with existing breathing complaints such as asthma, bronchitis or emphysema, are liable to be adversely affected by high concentrations ofparticulates. Particulates can also cause corrosion and soiling of metalwork or other materials, damage vegetation, and reduce visibility.

PM 10 Particles smaller than 10 microns (a micron is a millionth of a metre, or a thousandth of a millimetre) are called PM 10, and are not filtered out of the air by the nose, throat and upper windpipe.

As a result, these very small particles can enter the lungs where they may irritate or otherwise have an adverse effect on the delicate membranes and air sacs which absorb oxygen. Other toxic effects may occur, depending on the chemical make up of the fine particles.

Because they can enter the lungs, PM 10 particles are sometimes referred to as 'inhalable' particles, and are measured separately from TSP. Many health studies have concluded that lung function, cardio-respiratory mortality, respiratory illness-related hospital admissions, and a variety of other health factors are related to ambient concentrations of PM10.

However, which particular aspect of the fine particles is causing these effects has not yet been fully resolved. Particle chemistry, and possibly acidity, may be important. As for ozone, there appears to be no clearly defined "safe" threshold for PM10, or PM2.5.

Recent studies also suggest that particles have effects on the immune system (Wilson and Spengler, 1996; Blomberg, 1998). PM 10 and PM 2.5 have been declared "toxic" under the Canadian Environmental Protection Act (Environment Canada, 2000). This means that these substances must undergo a detailed review and actions must be put in place to reduce their production and release into the environment.

In Canada, only the Greater Vancouver Regional District (GVRD) and the province of Newfoundland have a standard in place for PM 10. In the United States, standards exist both nationally and in California, which has the same standard as the GVRD. PM 2.5 Another standard specification for measuring particulates is PM 2.5, which refers to particles equal to or smaller than 2.5 microns in size.

These particles are thought to be of special significance in terms of health impacts, as they have a higher chance of entering and remaining in the lungs if inhaled, compared to PM 10 or larger particles. They are sometimes referred to as 'respirable particles'.

Particulate matter in the PM 2.5 size range is emitted from industrial and domestic combustion sources including slash burning, industrial processes (e.g. power plants, pulp mills, mining, smelting, and refining), open fires, woodstoves, forest fires, and internal combustion engines of all kinds. PM 2.5 also forms when other air pollutants react together in the air.

An important chemical reaction leading to the production of PM 2.5 is the combination of sulphur dioxide with ammonia, producing ammonium sulphate. Many other reactions are possible between natural atmospheric components and the air pollutants typically emitted in populated regions of North America and the world in general. Particles produced by this "gas-to particle conversion" are very small and contribute to haze over large areas. Transportation, industrial and other fuel combustion account for about 25% of the PM 2.5 emitted to the air.

The rest comes from so-called "open" sources, which include open burning, forest fires, road dust and construction. The estimated emissions from road dust and forest fires are very large, and dominate the inventory. Emissions from some source sectors are of greater concern than others in terms of health and other environmental effects. Recent studies indicate that particulate from combustion sources is more "biologically active" than road or other dust from terrestrial sources. Diesel exhaust is of special concern as it is thought to contribute significantly to the risk of lung cancer (USEPA, 1999).

Numerous studies worldwide continue to find a significant association between PM 2.5 concentrations and a wide range of health effects, including premature mortality, many cardio-pulmonary symptoms, reduced activity, increased physician visits and other forms of disability.

Monitoring technologies were introduced in the mid 1990s which allow the continuous measurement of PM 10 or PM 2.5. These units provide continuous, unattended recording and electronic logging and reporting functions.

Volatile Organic Compounds

VOCs are carbon-containing substances which are present in the air in gas form, usually at low concentrations (in the parts per billion range). Used in the context of air quality, VOCs are substances which often evaporate readily. Thousands of different VOCs exist in the air. However, many VOCs are of natural origin, and in terms of environmental protection, the VOCs which cause some kind of problem are most important. Everyday examples of VOCs which may be a concern in the environment include gasoline and organic solvents.

Other products such as paint, adhesives, and a variety of other household goods may contain solvents which evaporate and contribute to the VOC content of the air. VOCs are also emitted by a wide range of industrial sources, as well as by motor vehicles. Vehicles emit VOCs in their exhaust, and from fuel tanks. Modern vehicles have systems in place to minimize such emissions, but overall, transport-related emissions are still substantial. A large number of VOCs can be emitted by industrial processes (for example by the petrochemicals or plastics industries).

Some VOCs may be potentially toxic to humans, animals or vegetation (e.g. benzene, 1,3 butadiene, ethylene) or are of concern because they can react in the air to form other harmful substances. For example, ethylene and propylene (and many other VOCs) may take part in reactions which lead to the formation of ozone-containing smog. Some VOCs, such as various petroleum hydrocarbons, may contribute to undesirable odours. The VOC sampling program in New Brunswick concentrates on about 150 compounds which are of special interest, including known and suspected carcinogens such as benzene and 1,3 butadiene, and photochemically active VOCs which contribute to smog formation.

3

Air Pollution, Sources and Characteristics

INTRODUCTION

Air pollution is the presence of substances in air in sufficient concentration and for sufficient time, so as to be, or threaten to be injurious to human, plant or animal life, or to property, or which reasonably interferes with the comfortable enjoyment of life and property.

Air pollutants arise from both man made and natural processes. Pollutants are also defined as primary pollutants resulting from combustion of fuels and industrial operations and secondary pollutants, those which are produced due to reaction of primary pollutants in the atmosphere.

The ambient air quality may be defined by the concentration of a set of pollutants which may be present in the ambient air we breath in. These pollutants may be called criteria pollutants. Emission standards express the allowable concentrations of a contaminant at the point of discharge before any mixing with the surrounding air.

COMBUSTION SOURCES

By combustion sources is meant operations where primarily fossil fuels, coal, natural gas, petrol, diesel and furnace oil are burnt to obtain energy. This includes power plants, industrial boilers, domestic heating and automobiles.

Thermal Power Pants

Thermal power plants are major sources of SPM, SO_2 and NO^x. Depending upon the type of fuel used, emission of one or more of these pollutants may be of environmental-significance. A large amount of SPM as fly ash is emitted from coal fired plants, particularly if the ash content of coal is high and a fly ash removal unit, such as, an electrostatic precipitation (ESP) is not used.

Oxides of nitrogen formed in combustion processes are usually due to either thermal fixation of atmospheric nitrogen in combustion air or to the conversion of chemically bound nitrogen in the fuel. Thermal fixation occurs when combustion temperature is above 1600°C. For natural gas and distillate oil nearly all NO results from thermal fixation. For residue oil and coal, the contribution to NO emission from fuel bound nitrogen may be significant.

The concentration of NO^x formed increases with increase in excess oxygen maintained in the combustion process and with the increase in temperature of the furnace. For coal based thermal power plants in India, it ranges between 100 and 200 mg/Nm^3 in the flue gas. In the case of natural gas and liquid fuels, the emission limits for flue gases prescribed in European countries is in the range of 200-400 mg/Nm^3.

AUTOMOBILES

In urban areas automobiles form a significant source of a number of air pollutants, namely, particulates, NO^x, hydrocarbons, carbon monoxide and lead. These pollutants are produced when fuel is burnt under less than ideal conditions. Non-uniform oxygen supply within the combustion chamber and lower flame temperature leads to incomplete combustion releasing CO, HC and unburnt particles in the exhaust. Tetraethyl lead, $(C^2H^5)^4$ Pb, is added to petrol as anti-knock additive. Where such petrol is used lead is emitted in the exhaust fumes as inorganic particulates.

INDUSTRIAL SOURCES

Only two sources are discussed here as illustrative examples.

Cement Manufacture

Raw materials include lime, silica, aluminum and iron. Lime is obtained from calcium carbonate. Other raw materials are introduced as sand, clay, shale, iron are and blast furnace slag. The process consist of mining, crushing, grinding, and calcining in a long cylindrically shaped oven or kiln. Air pollutants can originate at several operations as listed below.

Sulphuric Acid Manufacture

Sulphuric acid is produced from sulphur, which is burnt to obtain SO^2. Sulphur dioxide is converted to trioxide in presence of vanadium pentaoxide catalyst. The sulphur trioxide is absorbed in recycling concentrated sulfuric acid. Unreacted SO_2 escapes with the flue gas. New large plants now a days use double conversion double absorption (DCDA) process realizing above 99 percent efficiency.

CHARACTERISTICS

Major effects of some of the common pollutants are described in this section.

Suspended Particulate Matter

Atmospheric particulate matter is defined to be any dispersed matter, solid or liquid, smaller than, 500 μm. Under various conditions of their generation, they are also called by other names such as dust, fume, smoke and mist.

Dust usually refers to particles in the range of 1 to 200 μm size. Fume is very fine solid or liquid particles arising from chemical reactions or condensation of gases. Smoke refers to finely divided particles resulting from incomplete combustion of substances such as coal, petroleum, etc.

Particles in the range of 0.1μm to 10μm are of, most interest from health viewpoint. Particulate matter of less then 10μm size (PM10) is classified as respirable dust. Larger particles that enter the respiratory system are trapped by hairs and lining of nose or can be captured by mucus in upper respiratory tract and worked back to the throat by cilia and removed by spitting.

Particles between 0.5 and 10 μm, called thoracic particles, penetrate to the lungs and are deposited there. These particles by themselves and or by carrying other air pollutants adsorbed on them may cause the greatest harm. Elevated particulate concentrations in the atmosphere, in the range of 400 $\mu g/m^3$ and above especially in conjunction with oxides of sulphur have been linked to respiratory infections, bronchitis, asthma, pneumonia and the like. Many carbonaceous particles, especially those containing polycyclic aromatic hydrocarbons (PAH) are suspected carcinogens. Sulphur dioxide Sulphur dioxide when released in the atmosphere can also convert to SO_3, which leads to production of sulphuric acid. When SO_3 is inhaled it is likely to be absorbed in moist passages of respiratory tract. When it is entrained in an aerosol, however, it may reach far deeper into the lungs.

Sulphur dioxide can damage vegetation and cause corrosion. Airborne sulfates reduce visibility. It is also the cause of acid rain in some countries.

Nitrogen Oxides

Almost all NO^x emissions are in the form of NO, which has no known adverse health effects in the concentrations found in atmosphere. However, NO can be oxidized to NO_2 in the atmosphere, which in turn may give rise to secondary pollutants, which are injurious. NO_2 may also lead to formation of HNO_3, which is washed out of the atmosphere as acid rain.

Carbon Monoxide

Most of the CO emissions are from transportation sector. Peak concentrations occur at street level in busy urban centers particularly when there is no atmospheric mixing as it happens during winter season. Carbon monoxide interferes with blood's ability to carry oxygen. With the blood stream carrying less oxygen, brain function is affected and heart rate increases in an attempt to offset the oxygen deficit. Breathing between 20 to 35 ppm CO in air for 4 h results in impairment of time related response. Individuals with heart condition may experience chest pain. Exposure to 100ppm concentration would result in dizziness.

Lead

Lead released from motor vehicle exhaust may affect human populations by direct inhalation, in which case people living nearest to highways are at greatest risk. Lead can be ingested also after it is deposited on to foodstuffs. Measurements made in exposed communities indicate that lead concentration of 1 $\mu g/m^3$ in ambient air results in an increase of about 1-2 µg per decilitre (µg/dl) in blood. Lead poisoning can cause destructive behavioural changes, learning disabilities and permanent brain damage. Children and pregnant women are at greatest risk. Blood levels of 50-60 µg/dl are associated with neurobehavioural changes in children.

4

Air Pollutants and their Resources

Human exposure to pollutants within home exceeds the recommended limits set by the World Health Organisation (WHO). Unfortunately, indoor pollution has not been given much importance although most people spend as much as 80-90% of their time indoors.

The health effects from indoor air pollutants may be experienced soon after expo-sure or, possibly, years later.

INTRODUCTION

Many of us spend the greater part of our lives indoors. The indoor environment of homes and offices is often more seriously polluted than the outdoor atmosphere. Thus, for many people, the risks to health may be greater due to indoor air pollution than the outdoor air.

The major sources of indoor air pollution are those that release gases and particles into air, and inadequate ventilation makes the situation much worse.

The major factors that determine the quality of indoor air are:

- The nature of outdoor air quality around the building.
- The air exchange rate of the building (ventilation).
- The materials used in the construction of the building (presence of chemicals).

- The activities that go on inside the building (cleaning, cooking, heating etc.).
- Use of household chemicals.

INDOOR AIR AND YOUR HEALTH

In recent years, there have been an increasing number of com-plaints about the poor quality of indoor atmosphere from resi-dents, and workers in offices and commercial buildings. The pollutants found in indoor air are responsible for many harmful health effects. The effects may show up immediately after a single exposure, and include irritation of eyes, nose and throat, headache, dizziness and fatigue. Such immediate effects are usually of short duration and treatable. Sometimes the treat-ment is simply eliminating the person's exposure to the source of pollution. Symptoms of some diseases such as asthma, hyper-sensitivity, pneumonitis and humidifier fever may appear soon after exposure to certain indoor air pollutants. Though most of these diseases can be treated, nevertheless, some pose serious risks.

Other health problems may appear either years after a single exposure had occurred or on repeated exposures. These effects, which include some respiratory diseases, heart diseases and cancer, can be severely debilitating or fatal. Further research is needed to better understand the health hazards caused by expo-sure to average pollutant concentrations found in homes and those by higher concentrations that occur during short periods of time.

POLLUTANT SOURCES

There are many sources of indoor air pollution in a home. Most homes have more than one source that contribute to indoor air problems. Many activities go on inside a home which include cleaning, cooking, heating by open or enclosed fires, smoking, etc. Some important indoor air pollutants are generated by burning of oil, gas, kerosene, wood and tobacco products or produced by building materials, furnishings, wet or damp car-pets, household chemical products, air conditioners, dehumidi-fiers and outdoor sources such as radon and pesticides. Inad-equate ventilation can increase indoor pollutant level because of insufficient air movement to dilute emissions from indoor sources and carry them out of home.

RADIOACTIVITY

Most of the radioactivity inside a building is associated with radon, which is emitted from uranium in the soil or rock on which homes are built. Radon is a product of radioactive decay process beginning with uranium-238 and thorium-232. Be-cause of their longer half-lives (4.5 and 14 billion years respectively) they are present in trace quantities in many geological materials. Sometimes radon enters into the home through well water. Being a gas, radon escapes from construction material, penetrates through cracks in buildings and is released into the indoor atmosphere where it may be inhaled. The average indoor radon level is 1.3 pCi/l (pico curies per liter)

Volatile Organic Compounds (VOC)

There are many aliphatic and aromatic compounds contributing to VOC concentrations, with chloroform, acetone, chlorinated compounds and formaldehyde being predominant in many lo-cations. Consumer products used in homes contribute other VOCs to the indoor atmosphere. For example, latex paints contain toluene, ethylbenzene, 2-propanol and butane. Many organic compounds are emitted from construction materials, furnishings and consumer products such as latex paints, clean-ing agents, household solvents, detergents, waxes and varnishes. Formaldehyde in construction materials such as particle boards, plywood and in urea formaldehyde foam insulation, leaks into air when the temperature rises. Combined with other contami-nants it can cause headache, respiratory irritations, watery eyes, nausea, skin irritation and heart problems.

Indoor Combustion

Combustion of fuels such as oil, gas, kerosene, etc. inside a building contributes to the concentration of VOCs and it is also a source of stable inorganic gases. The common indoor pollut-ants due to combustion of fuels are particulate matter, oxides of nitrogen, oxides of sulphur, carbon monoxide, hydrocarbons and other odour causing chemicals. The emission quantity of these pollutants depends upon the type of fuel used, fuel / oxidant ratio and other combustion conditions. Proper venting of exhaust gases reduces this problem.

Tobacco Smoking

Tobacco smoke contains a complex mixture of over 4000 com-pounds, more than 40 of which are known to cause cancer, and as many are strong irritants.

Tobacco smoking is a source of VOCs including polyaromatic hydrocarbons (PAH), organic bases like nicotine, aldehydes, ketones, organic acids and respi-rable particulate matter. Smoking inside home is a cause for large amounts of indoor pollutants. Natural or mechanical ven-tilation techniques do not remove them from the air as quickly as they build up.

Cigarette smoking is another source of formaldehyde. The di-rectly inhaled air drawn through a cigarette may contain formal-dehyde concentrations more than 400 times the level of concen-tration in the indoor atmosphere. Tobacco smoking is responsible for approximately 3000 lung cancer deaths every year in non-smoking adults and causes respiratory infections in hundreds of thousands of children.

BIOLOGICAL CONTAMINANTS

Biological contaminants include pollens, bacteria, mildew, fun-gal spores, etc. There are many sources of these pollutants. Pollens originated from plants, and viruses and bacteria are transmitted by people and animals. Biological contaminants cause allergic diseases, pneumonitis, and some types of asthma. By controlling the relative humidity level (30-50 %) in a home, the growth of some of these sources of biological pollutants can be minimized.

PREVENTIVE MEASURES

Preventive measures for indoor air pollution in homes, apart-ments and offices involve eliminating or controlling the sources of pollution, increasing ventilation and installing air-cleaning devices.

Carefully choose building and furnishing materials (free from formaldehyde).

Ensure effective ventilation in all the areas of the building (good air exchange rate).

Install and use exhaust fans in kitchens and bathrooms.

Don't smoke at home or permit others to do so.

Use pesticides in recommended amounts with proper dilution.

Get air conditioners cleaned regularly.

Ensure cleanliness in the entire house especially in kitchens and bathrooms.

Get evaporation trays in dehumidifiers, air conditioners and refrigerators cleaned regularly. In gas stoves, a prescient yellow tipped flame is generally an indicator of maladjustment and increased pollutant emissions. Adjust the burner so that the flame tip is blue.

Keep exposure to products containing methylene chloride (paint stripper, adhesive remover) and benzene to a minimum.

Use high quality plywood in furnitures.

Some of the common indoor air pollutants, their sources and health effects are listed in the table.

Indoor air pollution is one of the major problems that we have to solve since we spend a large part of our life indoors. We should take all necessary precautions to eliminate or minimize the harmful effects of indoor air pollution.

DEFINITIONS OF AIR POLLUTION SOURCE CATEGORIES

Sources of air pollution like factories or cars are usually categorized by regulatory agencies into one of three groups: area, mobile, or point. Categorization of a specific source may vary depending on whether it is releasing "criteria" or "hazardous" air pollutants.

Criteria pollutants refer to six chemicals which occur frequently in ambient air and can injure human health, harm the environment or cause property damage: carbon monoxide, lead, nitrogen dioxide, ozone, particulate matter, and sulfur dioxide. Hazardous air pollutants (HAPs) refer to other chemicals which can cause adverse effects to human health or the environment. Congress has identifed over 188 of these pollutants, including substances that cause cancer, neurological, respiratory, and reproductive effects.

AREA SOURCES

Area sources include small pollution sources like dry cleaners, gas stations, and auto body paint shops. Area sources are defined as sources that emit less than 10 tons per year of a criteria or hazardous air pollutant or less than 25 tons per year of a combination of pollutants.

The category also includes commercial buildings (heating and cooling units; surface coatings), residential buildings (fire places; surface coatings), fuel combustion in non-road machinery, boats, railroads, and even the family lawnmower or barbecue grill. Waste disposal in the form of open burning, landfills and wastewater treatment are significant area sources.

Though emissions from individual area sources are relatively small, collectively their emissions can be of concern-particularly where large numbers of sources are located in heavily populated areas. Area sources are responsible for over 50% of particulate matter emissions and more than point or mobile sources for volatile organic compound (VOC) emissions, which contribute significantly to the formation of ground-level ozone.

MOBILE SOURCES

Mobile sources include both onroad vehicles (such as cars, trucks and buses) and offroad equipment (such as ships, airplanes, agricultural and construction equipment).

Mobile sources contribute significantly to air pollution. Driving a car is probably a person's single most polluting daily activity. Nationwide, mobile sources are responsible for about 75% of carbon monoxide pollution, and more oxides of nitrogen emissions than area or point sources. In urban areas, the motor vehicle contribution to carbon monoxide pollution can exceed 90 percent.

In a typical urban area, at least half of the hydrocarbon and nitrogen oxide pollutants come from mobile sources. Motor vehicles are also substantial sources of hazardous air pollutants, such as the recognized carcinogens benzene, formaldehyde, acetaldehyde, 1,3-butadiene and diesel particulate matter.

POINT SOURCES

Point sources include major industrial facilities like chemical plants, steel mills, oil refineries, power plants, and hazardous waste incinerators. Point sources are defined as those that emit 10 tons per year of any of the criteria pollutants or hazardous air pollutants or 25 tons per year of a mixture of air toxics. Nationwide, point sources like power plants, petroleum refineries, fertilizer manufacturers, industrial paper mills, copper smelters and iron and steel mills contribute the majority of sulfur dioxide emissions, accounting for nearly 90% of this criteria air pollutant. Point sources (predominantly electrical utilities and industrial boilers) are also major emitters of nitrogen oxides (NOx)-accounting for about 40% of total releases. Point sources are less important sources of VOCs-releasing less than 15% of total volatile organic compounds.

AREA SOURCES OF AIR POLLUTION

Area sources are smaller sources of air pollution, such as drycleaners, gas stations, etc. They often lack locational data and site-specific emissions data, so they are treated in exposure estimation models as sources that are distributed in space (i.e., releasing x tons of pollutant per square mile). Emissions levels from area sources are uncertain because they are often derived using various surrogates (such as levels of economic activity, etc.) The definitions of area sources for criteria and hazardous air pollutants are similar but not identical.

Area Sources-hazardous Air Pollutants

EPA's National-Scale Air Toxics Assessment defines area sources as pollution sources that generally have smaller emissions on an individual basis than major "point" sources and are often too small or ubiquitous in nature to be inventoried as individual sources. "Area sources" include facilities that have air toxics emissions below the major source threshold as defined in the air toxics sections of the Clean Air Act and thus emit less than 10 tons of a single toxic air pollutant or less than 25 tons of multiple toxic air pollutants in any one year. Area sources include smaller facilities, such as dry cleaners. "Other sources" include sources such as wildfires and prescribed burnings. NATA does not provide a breakout of more detailed area source categories. NATA does not include information on diesel emissions from point sources.

Area Sources-criteria Air Pollutants

Scorecard's criteria air pollutant reports are based on EPA's National Emissions Trends database. Definitions of EPA's area source category are provided in its National Air Pollutant Emissions Trends Report, 1900-1996.

To support Clean Air Act regulations, EPA has assigned Source Classification Categories (SCCs) for air pollution generating activities. These classifications are used to develop estimates and projections of air pollution by pollutant type. Presented below is a brief description of the area source categories used by Scorecard:

- *Stationary Source Fuel Combustion*: Industrial and electrical utilities, commercial, and institutional fuel combustion, residential fuel combustion (wood burning fires, gas and charcoal barbecue grills).
- *Industrial Processes*: Construction, mining and quarrying, in-process fuel use.
- *Solvent Utilization*: Surface coating operations, degreasing and commercial dry cleaning, auto body painting and refinishing.

- *Solvent Storage and Transport*: Organic chemical storage, petroleum storage and transport.
- *Waste Disposal, Treatment and Recovery*: Wastewater treatment, open burning and landfills.
- *Natural Sources*: Off-gasing from non-anthroprogenic sources (both biological and geologica).
- *Miscellaneous Area Sources*: Agricultural crop and livestock production, cooling towers and other combustion activities.

MOBILE SOURCES OF AIR POLLUTION

Mobile sources includes onroad vehicles (e.g., cars, trucks, buses) and offroad sources (e.g, airplanes, boats, and offroad equipment). Mobile sources emit both hazardous and criteria air pollutants, and are defined similarly by Clean Air Act regulatory programs targeting these different kinds of air pollution.

Mobile Sources-hazardous Air Pollutants

Scorecard's Hazardous Air Pollutant reports provide information about the amount of toxic chemicals mobile sources release in an area, as well as the resulting exposures and health risks. These reports are based on EPA's National-Scale Air Toxics Assessment, which splits mobile sources into two categories:

- *Onroad mobile sources*: Vehicles found on roads and highways (e.g., cars, trucks, buses).
- *Nonroad mobile sources*: Mobile sources not found on roads and highways (e.g., airplanes, trains, lawn mowers, construction vehicles, farm machinery).

Mobile Sources-criteria Air Pollutants

Scorecard's Criteria Air Pollutant reports provide information about the amount of criteria pollutants mobile sources release in an area, as well as the resulting exposures and health risks. These reports are based on EPA's National Emissions Trends database. Definitions of EPA's mobile source category are provided in its National Air Pollutant Emissions Trends Report, 1900-1996.

To support Clean Air Act regulations, EPA has assigned Source Classification Categories (SCCs) for air pollution generating activities.

These classifications are used to develop estimates and projections of air pollution by pollutant type. Scorecard's Criteria Air Pollutant reports define 'Mobile Sources' as sources with an SCC beginning with 'A22'. Presented below is a brief description of the mobile source categories used by Scorecard:

Highway Vehicles: Gasoline and diesel powered automobiles, buses and trucks.

Marine Vessels: Commercial, military and recreational.

Aircraft and Railroads

Paved and Unpaved Roads

Off-Road Equipment: Gasoline and diesel powered lawn and garden equipment, industrial and recreational engines.

EPA's Transportation and Air Quality program protects public health and the environment by regulating air pollution from motor vehicles, engines, and the fuels used to operate them, and by encouraging travel choices that minimize emissions.

These "mobile sources" include cars and light trucks, heavy trucks and buses, nonroad recreational vehicles (such as dirt bikes and snowmobiles), farm and construction machines, lawn and garden equipment, marine engines, aircraft, and locomotives. This program is managed by the Office of Transportation and Air Quality, which is part of EPA's Office of Air and Radiation.

TRANSPORTATION AND AIR QUALITY

- *Overview:* Pollutants and Programs: Information on how much air pollution and greenhouse gases are emitted by mobile sources, the programs OTAQ has undertaken to control these emissions, and the impact of those programs on air quality and climate change.
- *Consumer Information:* Learn what you can do to help reduce air pollution and how to buy the cleanest, most fuel-efficient vehicle that meets your needs.
- *Motor Vehicles and Engines:* Information about highway vehicles (cars and light trucks, heavy trucks, buses, engines, and motorcycles): fuel economy, emission standards and regulations, emission recall programs, new vehicle certification and in-use vehicle compliance, inspection and maintenance programs, diesel retrofit programs, evaluating the benefits of inventions designed to reduce emissions, and importing vehicles to the United States.
- *Nonroad Engines, Equipment, and Vehicles:* Information about aircraft, locomotives, diesel and gasoline boats and ships, personal watercraft, lawn and garden equipment, agricultural and construction machines, and recreational vehicles (such as dirt bikes and snowmobiles): emission standards and regulations, certification and compliance, and diesel retrofit programs.
- *Fuels and Fuel Additives:* Information on diesel, gasoline, and alternative fuels for mobile sources, fuel-quality control programs, requirements for registration and health effects testing of new fuels or fuel additives, and reporting forms.
- *Partnerships:* Information about our partnerships to reduce air pollution associated with transportation and other mobile sources. These programs include

commuter choice, diesel retrofit, buying a cleaner car or truck, and other initiatives.

- *State and Local Transportation Resources:* Information on the ties between land use, transportation planning, and air quality. Topics includes conformity, State Implementation Plans, transportation control measures, and available funding and grants for implementation of such programs.
- *Modeling, Testing, and Research:* Information on OTAQ models for estimating emissions from highway vehicles, nonroad sources, and fuels; how EPA tests and measures emissions; and OTAQ research into advanced technologies.

POINT SOURCES OF AIR POLLUTION

Point sources are large, stationary sources of air pollution, such as factories, power plants, etc. The definitions of point sources for criteria and hazardous air pollutants are similar but not identical.

Point Sources-hazardous Air Pollutants

EPA's National-Scale Air Toxics Assessment defines point sources as major stationary facilities that emit or have the potential to emit 10 tons of any one toxic air pollutant or 25 tons of more than one toxic air pollutant per year. NATA does not provide a breakout of more detailed point source categories. NATA also does not include information on diesel emissions from point sources.

Point Sources-criteria Air Pollutants

Scorecard's criteria air pollutant reports are based on EPA's National Emissions Trends database. Definitions of EPA's point source category are provided in its National Air Pollutant Emissions Trends Report, 1900-1996.

To support Clean Air Act regulations, EPA has assigned Source Classification Categories (SCCs) for air pollution generating activities. These classifications are used to develop estimates and projections of air pollution by pollutant type. Presented below is a brief description of the point source categories used by Scorecard:

- *External Combustion Boilers:* Electric utility power generation, industrial power generation.
- *Internal Combustion Engines:* Electrical generators, industrial power generators, commercial and institutional power generation, and engine testing operations.
- *Industrial Processes:* Chemical manufacturing, food and agricultural processes and primary metal production.
- *Petroleum and Solvent Evaporation:* Petroleum refining processes, surface coating operations, degreasing, industrial dry cleaning and organic chemical storage.
- *Waste Disposal:* Municipal solid waste disposal, commercial and institutional solid waste disposal, industrial solid waste incinerators including hazardous waste incinerators.
- *MACT Source Categories:* Food and agricultural processes, agricultural chemical production, styrene and methylacrylate production, use of cellulose based resins.

SOURCES OF AIR POLLUTION

Point Source Emissions

Point sources include industrial and nonindustrial stationary equipment or processes considered significant sources of air pollution emissions. A facility is considered to have significant emissions if it emits about one ton or more in a calendar year.

Examples of point sources include industrial and commercial boilers, electric-utility boilers, turbine engines, wood and pulp processers, paper mills, industrial surface coating facilities, refinery and chemical processing operations, and petroleum storage tanks. Area sources that may fall under the "point source" definition are piping leaks, industrial wastewater treatment ponds, rock and quarry operations, and tank farms. Insignificant point sources are included by category in the area source inventory.

The most accurate method for determining the amount of emissions produced by a facility is with continuous emissions monitoring. However, this is expensive and not always practicable. Emissions are estimated using a variety of methods.

Standard methods of estimating point source emissions are available from the U.S. Environmental Protection Agency in the Compilation of Air Pollutant Emission Factors, Volume I, also known as AP-42. Other methods include stack testing, equipment vendor test data, material balances such as for surface coating, or TCEQ-approved permit factors. If no other method is available, then the best engineering judgment must be used.

Facilities report point source emissions to the TCEQ for the calendar year and the data are stored in the Point Source Database. Data are available for use by TCEQ staff, the EPA, state and federal legislators, air pollution researchers, public interest groups and the general public.

EMISSIONS FROM NON-POINT SOURCES

On-Road Mobile Sources

Emissions from on-road mobile sources are estimated using a sophisticated model called MOBILE, which was developed by the EPA. MOBILE calculates an emissions factor for mobile sources using a set of complex mathematical equations that require several user input values.

Vehicles are segregrated into eight vehicle classes, with MOBILE generating an emissions factor for each class and a composite emissions factor representing all classes.

On-Road Mobile Source Vehicle Classes

- Light-duty gasoline vehicles (LDGV)
- Light-duty gasoline trucks up to 6,000 pounds gross vehicle weight (LDGT1)
- Light-duty gasoline trucks from 6,001 to 8,500 pounds gross vehicle weight (LDGT2)
- Heavy-duty gasoline vehicles with more than 8,500 pounds gross vehicle weight (HDGV)
- Light-duty diesel vehicles (LDDV)
- Heavy-duty diesel vehicles with more than 8,500 pounds gross vehicle weight (HDDV)
- Motorcycles (MC)
- Light-duty diesel-powered trucks (LDDI)

After an emissions factor is generated for each vehicle class, the factor is then used in conjunction with the vehicle miles traveled (VMT) estimates, which were developed with the Texas Highway Performance Monitoring System (HPMS) data set for that selected area. This combination determines the contribution of emissions from mobile sources in a city, county, or state. VMT data is maintained by the Texas Department of Transportation.

The HPMS Program produces VMT estimates for various roadway types categorized into two major population areas-urban and rural.

Roadway Types

Urban	**Rural**
Interstate	Interstate
Other freeways and expressways	Other principal arterial
Other principal arterial	Minor arterial
Minor arterial	Major collector
Collector	Minor collector
Local	Local

In Texas, emissions from mobile sources are estimated on a county-wide basis. With a few exceptions nationwide, on-road mobile sources constitute the largest single source category of air pollution.

Non-Road Mobile Sources

- Non-Road Mobile Source Emissions Data

Nonroad mobile sources include a wide variety of internal combustion engines not associated with highway vehicles. Emissions calculation methodology is as varied as the categories themselves. A federal computer model using engine types and landing-takeoff cycles is used to calculate most aircraft emissions. Actual fuel usage and track mileage are applied to determine locomotive emissions. Data on ship and barge traffic is used to calculate emissions from ocean vessels.

Nonroad Mobile Source Categories

Aircraft:	**Small Engines:**
Commercial	Lawn and garden
Military	Airport support vehicles
	Recreational marine
General:	Light commercial
Locomotives	Industrial construction
Vessels (ships and barges)	Agricultural logging

The EPA developed emissions factors for a lengthy list of small engine categories, which included research on individual engines and fuel types. Included in this category are two major emissions sources-lawn mowers and recreational boat engines.

Nonroad Mobile Small Engine Categories

Lawn and Garden:

Trimmers/edgers/brush cutters

Lawn mowers

Leaf blowers/vacuums

Rear engine riding mowers

Front mowers

Chainsaws, 4 horsepower (HP)

Shredders, 5 HP

Tillers, 5 HP

Lawn and garden tractors

Wood splitters

Snowblowers

Chippers/stump grinders

Commercial turf equipment

Other lawn and garden equipment

Airport Support:

Aircraft support equipment

Terminal tractors

Recreational Vehicles:

All terrain vehicles

Minibikes

Off-road motorcycles

Golf carts

Snowmobiles

Specialty vehicle carts

Recreational Marine:

Vessels with inboard engines
Vessels with outboard engines
Vessels with stern drive engines
Sailboat auxiliary inboard engines
Sailboat auxiliary outboard engines

Light Commercial:

Generator sets, 50 HP
Pumps, 50 HP
Air compressors, 50 HP
Gas compressors, 50 HP
Welders, 50 HP
Pressure washers, 50 HP

Industrial:

Aerial Lifts
Forklifts
Sweepers/scrubbers
Other general industrial equipment
Other material handling equipment

Construction:

Asphalt pavers
Tampers/rammers
Plate compactors
Concrete pavers
Rollers
Scrapers
Paving equipment
Surfacing equipment
Signal boards
Trenchers
Bore/drill rigs
Excavators

Concrete/industrial Saws
Cement and mortar mixers
Cranes
Graders
Off-highway trucks
Crushing/process equipment
Rough terrain forklifts
Rubber tired loaders
Rubber tired dozers
Tractors/loaders/backhoes
Crawler tractors
Skid steer loaders
Off-highway tractors
Dumpers/tenders
Other construction equipment

Agricultural:

2-wheel tractors
Agricultural tractors
Agricultural mowers
Combines
Sprayers
Balers
Tillers, 5 HP
Swathers
Hydro power units
Other agricultural equipment

Logging:

Chainsaws, 4 HP
Shredders, 5 HP
Skidders
Fellers/bunchers

Area Sources

Area Source Emissions Data: Area source inventories generally report emissions by categories rather than by individual source; a common method in reporting point source emissions. Area source emissions are calculated by various methods and depend on the type of data available for each category. For example, whenever fuel use and materials data are not available, employee and county population numbers are used with established emission factors to calculate emissions. Emissions are calculated and reported on a county-wide basis.

Major categories of area sources are:

- Stationary source fuel combustion such as residential fuel combustion
- Solvent use (e.g., small surface coating operations)
- Product storage and transport distribution (e.g., gasoline)
- Light industrial/commercial sources
- Agriculture (e.g., feedlots, crop burning)
- Waste management (e.g., landfills)
- Miscellaneous area sources (e.g., forest fires, wind erosion, unpaved roads)

The following table gives a more complete list of area sources by category.

Product Storage and Transport Distribution:

Oil and gas production

Oil and gas production-offshore

Aircraft refueling

Marine vessel loading losses

Leaking underground tanks

Catastrophic/accidental releases

Service Stations:

Vehicle refueling

Tank truck unloading

Tank trucks in transit

Tank breathing losses

Other (spillage)

Solvent Use:

Barge, tank, tank truck, rail car, drum cleaning

Consumer/commercial solvent use

Surface cleaning (degreasing)

Dry cleaning

Graphic arts

Cutback asphalt

Emulsified asphalt

Waste management:

Municipal waste landfills

Municipal wastewater treatment (POTW)

Industrial wastewater treatment

Wastewater package plants

Light Industrial and Commercial Sources:

Commercial bakeries

Breweries

Wineries

Distilleries

Agriculture and Miscellaneous Area Sources:

Pesticide application

Orchard heaters

Agricultural burning

Prescribed burning

Structure fires

Forest fires

Slash burning
Open burning

Painting Operations:

Architectural coatings
Auto refinishing
Traffic markings
Furniture fixtures
Metal containers
Automobiles (new)
Machinery and equipment
Appliances
Other transportation equipment
Sheet, strip, and coil
Factory finished wood
Electrical insulation
Other product coatings
High-performance maintenance
Marine coatings
Other special purpose coatings

Stationary Source Fuel Combustion:

Fuel oil-residential
Fuel oil-commercial/distillate
Fuel oil-commercial/residual
Fuel oil-industrial/residual
Coal-residential
Coal-commercial
Coal-industrial
Natural gas-residential
Natural gas-commercial
Natural gas-industrial
LPG-residential
LPG-commercial

LPG-industrial
Wood-residential

BIOGENIC SOURCES

Biogenic emissions account for 30 percent of all the volatile organic compounds (VOCs) emitted in urban areas in the eastern half of Texas. For the purposes of photochemical modeling, biogenic VOC emissions are estimated using a computer model that takes into account the species of trees present, the density of their foliage, the temperature and solar radiation on the day in question, and the distribution of vegetation throughout the modeling domain.

It is important to measure these parameters accurately if the biogenics inventory is to be correct. The TCEQ has hired specialists to measure some of these variables in north-central and southeastern Texas.

Most plants emit some VOCs, but the largest emitters are oaks, pines, sweet gums, eucalypti, and poplars. Some VOCs are easily detected by their aroma. Pines, sycamores, and eucalypti emit fragrant monoterpenes, while other VOCs-such as isoprene-are not as aromatic.

Isoprene is a byproduct of photosynthesis. Scientists still debate the purpose of its emission but some evidence suggests that plants can cope better with heat if isoprene is present. Because it is generated by photosynthesis, isoprene emissions are not generated at night.

Monoterpenes are known as "essential oils." There is solid evidence that plants make monoterpenes, which are found in small reservoirs in the leaves or needles of plants, to ward off herbivores.

When an insect feeds on the leaf, the monoterpenes are released and can adversely affect the insect's health. Because the monoterpenes are always present in the leaves, their emission rate depends mostly on the temperature. Higher temperatures will evaporate larger amounts into the atmosphere.

There are a few other important organic compounds emitted by plants. Alcohols are often emitted by damaged vegetation; there is some evidence that these alcohols act as an antiseptic. A few recent studies suggest that alkenes are also emitted by some plants.

GREENHOUSE EFFECT

A schematic representation of the exchanges of energy between outer space, the Earth's atmosphere, and the Earth surface. The ability of the atmosphere to capture and recycle energy emitted by the Earth surface is the defining characteristic of the greenhouse effect.

The greenhouse effect is the process in which the emission of infrared radiation by the atmosphere warms a planet's surface. The name comes from an incorrect analogy with the warming of air inside a greenhouse compared to the air outside the greenhouse. The greenhouse effect was discovered by Joseph Fourier in 1824 and first investigated quantitatively by Svante Arrhenius in 1896.

The Earth's average surface temperature of 15 °C (59 °F) is about 33 °C (59 °F) warmer than it would be without the greenhouse effect.[2] Global warming, a recent warming of the Earth's lower atmosphere, is believed to be the result of an enhanced greenhouse effect due to increased concentrations of greenhouse gases in the atmosphere. In addition to the Earth, Mars and Venus have greenhouse effects.

BASIC MECHANISM

The Earth receives energy from the Sun in the form of radiation. Most of the energy is in visible wavelengths and in infrared wavelengths that are near the visible range (often called "near infrared"). The Earth reflects about 30% of the incoming solar radiation. The remaining 70% is absorbed, warming the land, atmosphere and oceans.

For the Earth's temperature to be in steady state so that the Earth does not rapidly heat or cool, this absorbed solar radiation must be very closely balanced by energy radiated back to space in the infrared wavelengths. Since the intensity of infrared radiation increases with increasing temperature, one can think of the Earth's temperature as being determined by the infrared flux needed to balance the absorbed solar flux.

The visible solar radiation mostly heats the surface, not the atmosphere, whereas most of the infrared radiation escaping to space is emitted from the upper atmosphere, not the surface. The infrared photons emitted by the surface are mostly absorbed in the atmosphere by greenhouse gases and clouds and do not escape directly to space.

The reason this warms the surface is most easily understood by starting with a simplified model of a purely radiative greenhouse effect that ignores energy transfer in the atmosphere by convection (sensible heat transport) and by the evaporation and condensation of water vapor (latent heat transport). In this purely radiative case, one can think of the atmosphere as emitting infrared radiation both upwards and downwards. The upward infrared flux emitted by the surface must balance not only the absorbed solar flux but also this downward infrared flux emitted by the atmosphere. The surface temperature will rise until it generates thermal radiation equivalent to the sum of the incoming solar and infrared radiation.

A more realistic picture taking into account the convective and latent heat fluxes is somewhat more complex. But the following simple model captures the essence. The starting point is to note that the opacity of the atmosphere to infrared radiation determines the height in the atmosphere from which most of the photons are emitted into space. If the atmosphere is more opaque, the typical photon escaping to space will be emitted from higher in the atmosphere, because one then has to go to higher altitudes to see out to space in the infrared. Since the emission of infrared radiation is a function of temperature, it is the temperature of the atmosphere at this emission level that is effectively determined by the requirement that the emitted flux balance the absorbed solar flux.

But the temperature of the atmosphere generally decreases with height above the surface, at a rate of roughly 6.5 °C per kilometer on average, until one reaches the stratosphere 10-15 km above the surface. (Most infrared photons escaping to space are emitted by the troposphere, the region bounded by the surface and the stratosphere, so we can ignore the stratosphere in this simple picture.)

A very simple model, but one that proves to be remarkably useful, involves the assumption that this temperature profile is simply fixed, by the non-radiative energy fluxes. Given the temperature at the emission level of the infrared flux escaping to space, one then computes the surface temperature by increasing temperature at the rate of 6.5 °C per kilometer, the environmental lapse rate, until one reaches the surface.

The more opaque the atmosphere, and the higher the emission level of the escaping infrared radiation, the warmer the surface, since one then needs to follow this lapse rate over a larger distance in the vertical. While less intuitive than the purely radiative greenhouse effect, this less familiar radiative-convective picture is the starting point for most discussions of the greenhouse effect in the climate modeling literature.

The term "greenhouse effect" is a source of confusion in that actual greenhouses do not warm by this mechanism (see section Real greenhouses). Popular discussions often imply incorrectly that they do; this error is sometimes made even in materials from scientific or governmental agencies (e.g., the U.S. Environmental Protection Agency).

Greenhouse Gases

Quantum mechanics provides the basis for computing the interactions between molecules and radiation. Most of this interaction occurs when the frequency of the radiation closely matches that of the spectral lines of the molecule, determined by the quantization of the modes of vibration and rotation of the molecule. (The electronic excitations are generally not relevant for infrared radiation, as they require energy larger than that in an infrared photon.)

The width of a spectral line is an important element in understanding its importance for the absorption of radiation. In the Earth's atmosphere these spectral widths are primarily determined by "pressure broadening", which is the distortion of the spectrum due to the collision with another molecule. Most of the infrared absorption in the atmosphere can be thought of as occurring while two molecules are colliding. The absorption due to a photon interacting with a lone molecule is relatively small.

This three-body aspect of the problem, one photon and two molecules, makes direct quantum mechanical computation for molecules of interest more challenging. Careful laboratory spectroscopic measurements, rather than ab initio quantum mechanical computations, provide the basis for most of the radiative transfer calculations used in studies of the atmosphere.

The molecules/atoms that constitute the bulk of the atmosphere: oxygen (O_2), nitrogen (N_2) and argon (Ar); do not interact with infrared radiation significantly. While the oxygen and nitrogen molecules can vibrate, because of their symmetry these vibrations do not create any transient charge separation. Without such a transient dipole moment, they can neither absorb nor emit infrared radiation. In the Earth's atmosphere, the dominant infrared absorbing gases are water vapor, carbon dioxide, and ozone (O_3). The same molecules are also the dominant infrared emitting molecules. CO_2 and O_3 have "floppy" vibration motions whose quantum states can be excited by collisions at energies encountered in the atmosphere.

For example, carbon dioxide is a linear molecule, but it has an important vibrational mode in which the molecule bends with the carbon in the middle moving one way and the oxygens on the ends moving the other way, creating some charge separation, a dipole moment, thus carbon dioxide molecules can absorb IR radiation.

Collisions will immediately transfer this energy to heating the surrounding gas. On the other hand, other CO_2 molecules will be vibrationally excited by collisions. Roughly 5% of CO_2 molecules are vibrationally excited at room temperature and it is this 5% that radiates. A substantial part of the greenhouse effect due to carbon dioxide exists because this vibration is easily excited by infrared radiation. CO_2 has two other vibrational modes.

The symmetric stretch does not radiate, and the asymmetric stretch is at too high a frequency to be effectively excited by atmospheric temperature collisions, although it does contribute to absorption of IR radiation.

The vibrational modes of water are at too high energies to effectively radiate, but do absorb higher frequency IR radiation. Water vapor has a bent shape. It has a permanent dipole moment (the O atom end is electron rich, and the H atoms electron poor) which means that IR light can be emitted and absorbed during rotational transitions, and these transitions can also be produced by collisional energy transfer. Clouds are also very important infrared absorbers. Therefore, water has multiple effects on infrared radiation, through its vapor phase and through its condensed phases. Other absorbers of significance include methane, nitrous oxide and the chlorofluorocarbons.

Discussion of the relative importance of different infrared absorbers is confused by the overlap between the spectral lines due to different gases, widened by pressure broadening. As a result, the absorption due to one gas cannot be thought of as independent of the presence of other gases. One convenient approach is to remove the chosen constituent, leaving all other absorbers, and the temperatures, untouched, and monitoring the infrared radiation escaping to space.

The reduction in infrared absorption is then a measure of the importance of that constituent. More precisely, define the greenhouse effect (GE) to be the difference between the infrared radiation that the surface would radiate to space if there were no atmosphere and the actual infrared radiation escaping to space. Then compute the percentage reduction in GE when a constituent is removed. The table below is computed by this method, using a particular 1-dimensional model of the atmosphere. More recent 3D computations lead to similar results.

Gas removed	**percent reduction in GE**
H_2O	36%
CO_2	9%
O_3	3%

(**Source:** GISS-GCM ModelE simulation)

By this particular measure, water vapor can be thought of as providing 36% of the greenhouse effect, and carbon dioxide 9%, but the effect of removal of both of these constituents will be greater than the total that each reduces the effect, in this case more than 45%. An additional proviso is that these numbers are computed holding the cloud distribution fixed. But removing water vapor from the atmosphere while holding clouds fixed is not likely to be physically relevant. In addition, the effects of a given gas are typically nonlinear in the amount of that gas, since the absorption by the gas at one level in the atmosphere can remove photons that would otherwise interact with the gas at another altitude. The kinds of estimates presented in the table, while often encountered in the controversies surrounding global warming, must be treated with caution. Different estimates found in different sources typically result from different definitions and do not reflect uncertainties in the underlying radiative transfer.

Positive Feedback and Runaway Greenhouse Effect

When there is a loop of effects such as the concentration of a greenhouse gas itself being a function of temperature, there is a feedback. If the effect is to act in the same direction on temperature it is a positive feedback; and if in the opposite direction it is a negative feedback. Sometimes feedback effects can be on the same cause as the forcing but it can also be via another greenhouse gas or on other effects such as change in ice cover affecting the planet's albedo.

Positive feedbacks do not have to lead to a runaway effect. With radiation from the Earth increasing in proportion to the fourth power of temperature, the feedback effect has to be very strong to cause a runaway effect. An increase in temperature from greenhouse gases leading to increased water vapour which is a greenhouse gas causing further warming is a positive feedback. This cannot be a runaway effect or the runaway effect would have occurred long ago. Positive feedback effects are common and can always exist while runaway effects are much rarer and cannot be operating at all times.

If the effects from the second iteration of the loop of effects is larger than the effects of the first iteration of the loop this will lead to a self perpetuating effect. If this occurs and the feedback only ends after producing a major temperature increase, it is called a runaway greenhouse effect. A runaway feedback could also occur in the opposite direction leading to an ice age. Runaway feedbacks are bound to stop, since infinite temperatures are not observed. They are allowed to stop due to things like a reducing supply of a greenhouse gas or a phase change of the gas or ice cover reducing towards zero or increasing toward a large size that is difficult to increase.

According to the clathrate gun hypothesis a runaway greenhouse effect could be caused by liberation of methane gas from hydrates by global warming if there are sufficient hydrates close to unstable conditions. It has been speculated that the Permian-Triassic extinction event was caused by such a runaway effect. It is also thought that large quantities of methane could be released from the Siberian tundra as it begins to thaw, methane being 21-times more potent a greenhouse gas than carbon dioxide.

A runaway greenhouse effect involving CO_2 and water vapor may have occurred on Venus. On Venus today there is little water vapor in the atmosphere. If water vapor did contribute to the warmth of Venus at one time, this water is thought to have escaped to space. Venus is sufficiently strongly heated by the Sun that water vapor can rise much higher in the atmosphere and is split into hydrogen and oxygen by ultraviolet light. The hydrogen can then escape from the atmosphere and the oxygen recombines. Carbon dioxide, the dominant greenhouse gas in the current Venusian atmosphere, likely owes its larger concentration to the weakness of carbon recycling as compared to Earth, where the carbon dioxide emitted from volcanoes is efficiently subducted into the Earth by plate tectonics on geologic time scales.

Anthropogenic Greenhouse Effect

CO_2 production from increased industrial activity (fossil fuel burning) and other human activities such as cement production and tropical deforestation has increased the CO_2 concentrations in the atmosphere. Measurements of carbon dioxide amounts from Mauna Loa observatory show that CO_2 has increased from about 313 ppm (parts per million) in 1960 to about 375 ppm in 2005. The current observed amount of CO_2 exceeds the geological record of CO_2 maxima (~300 ppm) from ice core data.

Because it is a greenhouse gas, elevated CO_2 levels will increase global mean temperature; based on an extensive review of the scientific literature, the Intergovernmental Panel on Climate Change concludes that "most of the observed increase in globally averaged temperatures since the mid-20th century is very likely due to the observed increase in anthropogenic greenhouse gas concentrations".

Over the past 800,000 years, ice core data shows unambiguously that carbon dioxide has varied from values as low as 180 parts per million (ppm) to the pre-industrial level of 270ppm. Certain paleoclimatologists consider variations in carbon dioxide to be a fundamental factor in controlling climate variations over this time scale.

Real Greenhouses

The term 'greenhouse effect' originally came from the greenhouses used for gardening, but it is a misnomer since greenhouses operate differently. A greenhouse is built of glass. It heats up mainly because the Sun warms the ground inside it and this warms the air in the greenhouse. The air continues to heat because it is confined within the greenhouse, unlike the environment outside the greenhouse where warm air near the surface rises and mixes with cooler air aloft. This can be demonstrated by opening a small window near the roof of a greenhouse: the temperature will drop considerably. It has also been demonstrated experimentally (Wood, 1909): a "greenhouse" built of rock salt (which is transparent to infrared radiation) heats up just as one built of glass does.

Greenhouses thus work primarily by preventing convection; the atmospheric greenhouse effect however reduces radiation loss, not convection. It is quite common, however, to find sources that make the erroneous "greenhouse" analogy. Although the primary mechanism for warming greenhouses is the prevention of mixing with the free atmosphere, the radiative properties of the glazing can still be important to commercial growers. With the modern development of new plastic surfaces and glazings for greenhouses, this has permitted construction of greenhouses which selectively control radiation transmittance in order to better control the growing environment.

AUTOMOBILE EMISSIONS CONTROL

Automobile emissions control covers all the technologies that are employed to reduce the air pollution-causing emissions produced by automobiles. Exhaust emissions control systems were first required on 1966 model year vehicles produced for sale in the state of California, followed by the United States as a whole in model year 1968. Their use became widespread in the following decades and now they are ubiquitous in industrialized nations and common in most others.

Emissions controls have been highly successful in reducing the emissions produced by motor vehicles in terms of quantity per distance traveled. However, substantial increases in the distance traveled by each vehicle, and equally substantial increases in the number of vehicles in use, have meant that the overall reduction in pollution has been much slower.

The emissions produced by a vehicle fall into three basic categories:

- *Tailpipe Emissions:* This is what most people think of when they think of vehicle air pollution; the products of burning fuel in the vehicle's engine, emitted from the vehicle's exhaust system. The major pollutants emitted include:
  1. *Hydrocarbons:* this class is made up of unburned or partially burned fuel, and is a major contributor to urban smog, as well as being toxic. They can cause liver damage and even cancer.
  2. *Nitrogen Oxides (NOx):* These are generated when nitrogen in the air reacts with oxygen under the high temperature and pressure conditions inside the engine. NOx emissions contribute to both smog and acid rain.
  3. *Carbon Monoxide (CO):* a product of incomplete combustion, carbon monoxide reduces the blood's ability to carry oxygen and is dangerous to people with heart disease.
  4. *Carbon Dioxide (CO_2):* Emissions of carbon dioxide are an increasing concern as its role in global warming as a greenhouse gas has become more apparent.
- *Evaporative Emissions:* These are produced from the evaporation of fuel, and are a large contributor to urban smog, since these heavier molecules stay closer to ground level. Fuel tends to evaporate in these ways:

1. *Gas Tank Venting*: the heating of the vehicle as the temperature rises from the night-time temperature to the hottest temperatures of the day mean that gasoline in the tank evaporates, increasing the pressure inside the tank above atmospheric pressure. This pressure must be relieved, and before emissions control it was simply vented into the atmosphere.
2. *Running Losses*: the escape of gasoline vapors from the hot engine.
3. *Refuelling Losses*: these can cause a lot of hydrocarbon vapor emission. The empty space inside a vehicle's tank is filled with hydrocarbon gases, and as the tank is filled, these gases are forced out into the atmosphere. In addition, there is loss from further evaporation and fuel spillage.

- *Life Cycle Emissions:* These are produced in activities associated with the manufacturing, maintenance, and disposal of the automobile and include such items as:
  1. Manufacturing plant power requirements
  2. Volatile solvents utilized in the manufacturing process (auto paint finishes, etc)
  3. Outgassing of synthetic materials utilized to reduce weight and simplify manufacturing
  4. Maintenance requirements such as oil and filter changes, battery replacement, etc.
  5. Disposal requirements including contaminated lubricants, tires, heavy metals, and landfill

Tailpipe Emissions Control

Tailpipe emissions control can be categorised into three parts:

1. Increasing engine efficiency
2. Increasing vehicle efficiency
3. Cleaning up the emissions

Increasing Engine Efficiency

Engine efficiency has been gradually improved with progress in following technologies:

- Electronic ignition
- Fuel injection systems
- Electronic control unit

Increasing Vehicle Efficiency

Contributions to the goal of reducing fuel consumption and related emissions come from

- lightweight vehicle design
- minimized air resistance
- reduced rolling resistance
- improved powertrain efficiency
- increasing spark to the spark plug (this topic should be under the ignition system)
- regenerative braking

Each of these items breaks down into a number of factors.

Increasing Driving Efficiency

Significant reduction of emissions come from

- driving technique (some 10-30% reduction)
- unobstructed traffic conditions
- cruising at an optimum speed for the vehicle
- reducing the number of cold starts

Cleaning up the Emissions

Advances in engine and vehicle technology continually reduce the amount of pollutants generated, but this is generally considered insufficient to meet emissions goals. Therefore, technologies to react with and clean up the remaining emissions have long been an essential part of emissions control.

Air Injection

A very early emissions control system, the Air injection reactor (AIR) reduces the products of incomplete combustion (hydrocarbons and carbon monoxide) by injecting fresh air into the exhaust manifolds of the engine. In the presence of this oxygen-laden air, further combustion occurs in the manifold and exhaust pipe.

Generally the air is delivered through an engine-driven 'smog pump' and air tubing to the manifolds. This technology was introduced in 1966 in California, and was in use for the next several decades. It is not generally in use any longer, having been supplanted by cleaner burning engines and better catalytic converters.

Exhaust Gas Recirculation

Many engines produced after the 1973 model year have an exhaust gas recirculation valve between the exhaust and intake manifolds; its sole purpose is to reduce NOx emissions by introducing exhaust gases into the air/fuel mixture, lowering peak combustion temperatures.

Around 1990, the Jeep division's powerplants (2.5 and 4.0) eliminated the EGR system. Some other engines also have dispensed with EGR, such as GM's Ecotec engine which was able to meet LEV emissions standards without requiring EGR. In some cases, the valve timing has been set to hold some exhaust in the combustion chamber after the exhaust stroke to perform a similar function to EGR.

Catalytic Converters

The catalytic converter is a device, placed in the exhaust pipe, which converts various emissions into less harmful ones using, generally, a combination of platinum, palladium and rhodium as catalysts. Catalytic converters have been steadily improved over the years.

They make for a significant, and easily applied, method for reducing tailpipe emissions. Their other significant effect on pollution was that they were incompatible with the use of tetraethyl lead as an octane booster in gasoline, prompting the phasing-out of that additive as converter-fitted cars became more prevalent. The lead emissions were highly damaging to human health, and its virtual elimination has been one of the most successful reductions in air pollution.

Evaporative Emissions Control

Efforts at the reduction of evaporative emissions include the capturing of vented vapors from within the vehicle, and the reduction of refuelling emissions.

Capturing Vented Vapors

Within the vehicle, vapors from the fuel tank are channelled through canisters containing activated carbon instead of being vented to the atmosphere. These are known as carbon canisters. The vapors are adsorbed within the canister, which feeds into the inlet manifold of the engine. When the vehicle is running, the vapors desorb from the carbon, are drawn into the engine and burned.

Evaporative emissions from the vehicle are limited by law and tested as part of the new vehicle type approval by a so-called SHED-test. The current limit in the USA is 2 grams of HC per hour, which may amount to an evaporation of one liter (1/4 gallon) in a month.

Reducing Refueling Losses

All modern vehicles have tank filler necks that instead of just being a tube into the tank, as in earlier vehicles, now have a small-diameter hinged and spring-loaded door only large enough for the tip of the filler nozzle. This prevents vapor leakage when the filler cap is removed, and also prevents a catalytic converter-fitted vehicle being refueled with leaded fuel (since the leaded fuel nozzle is too large to fit).

This is accompanied by modifications to the filling station pumps. They are now equipped to suck the vapors back into the pump as they are displaced by fuel. Some have intakes around the head of the filler nozzle, while others have a rubber 'boot' that presses securely around the end of the filler neck to prevent vapors escaping.

Vehicles sold in North America started to be equipped with "onboard refueling vapor recovery" (ORVR) systems around 1997. These systems are designed to capture the vapors displaced by the incoming fuel and evaporated by high environmental temperatures in the vehicle's vapor canister rather than releasing them into the atmosphere. This system makes vapor recovery systems on filling station pumps redundant.

Emission Testing

In 1966, the first emission test cycle was enacted in the State of California measuring tailpipe emissions in PPM (parts per million). The most common test used until the 1980s was the idle test (usually a two-speed idle test), later to be succeeded with a dynamometer (the latest variant is known as the accelerated simulated mode, ASM for short).

ASM testing tests for three gases instead of two; if one gas emission is higher, the vehicle fails the test. Usually, vehicles under 10,000 GVW and gasoline powered are subjected to ASM testing with the exemption of all-wheel drive vehicles (including full-time four wheel drive), and vehicles at or over 25 years of age having undergone a visual inspection.

The Environmental Working Group used California ASM emissions data to create an Auto Asthma Index that rates vehicle models based on emissions of hydrocarbons and nitrogen oxides, the chemicals that create smog.

Some cities are also using a technology developed by Donald H. Stedman, PhD. (a chemistry professor at the University of Denver) which uses lasers to detect emissions while vehicles pass by on public roads, thus eliminating the need for owners to go to a test center. Stedman's laser detection of exhaust gases is the progenitor of remote sensing devices-commonly used in metropolitan areas.

By the early 1990s after the passage of the Clean Air Act of 1990, stricter testing criteria was phased in; the EPA introduced the IM240 testing. Around 35 states (as of this writing) have phased in I/M (inspection/maintenance) criteria modeled after the California Air Resources Board's emission testing standard.

California emission testing laws were amended in 1998 when SB 42 was passed-a new criteria phased in was the rolling chassis exemption to which vehicle manufactured between 1973-1998 were subjected to emission testing. This law was reversed last year by California governor Arnold Schwarznegger where the rolling chassis exemption was repealed; as of 2005, 1976 and newer vehicles are subject to testing.

In Ireland emission testing is covered by the NCT bi-annual test for private vehicles and the yearly DOE (Dept. Of Environment) for commercial vehicles.

EMISSION STANDARD

Emission standards are requirements that set specific limits to the amount of pollutants that can be released into the environment. Many emission standards focus on regulating pollutants released by automobiles (motor cars) and other powered vehicles but they can also regulate emissions from industry, power plants, small equipment such as lawn mowers and diesel generators. Frequent policy alternatives to emission standards are technology standards (which mandate the use of a specific technology) and emission trading.

Standards generally regulate the emissions of NOx, sulfur oxides, particulate matter (PM) or soot, carbon monoxide (CO), or volatile hydrocarbons (see carbon dioxide equivalent).

Vehicles and CO_2

The main components of automobile exhaust are nitrogen (N_2), carbon dioxide (CO_2), and water vapor (H_2O). Carbon dioxide is the most important anthropogenic greenhouse gas (GHG) and the most significant Greenhouse Gas emitted in the U.S. (with 82-84% of all U.S. emissions). Increases in carbon dioxide concentration are due primarily to fossil fuel use and land-use change.

The 700 million cars currently on the world's roads produce 2.8 billion tons of CO_2 annually. This represents 20% of the world's CO_2 emissions.

The CO_2 emission standards can be referred to the fuel or to the vehicle :

- The European Union is moving towards fuel mandatory CO_2 standards and USA has reflected it in the Greenhouse Gas Score.
- There are information, but mandatory, standards for CO2 limits in vehicle (engine) emissions, excepting

some concrete or state regulations (e.g. CAFE or California Air Resources Board).

CO_2 mass emission in vehicles is measured in g/km (g/mi * 0.621371192 = g/km).

Low Carbon Fuel Standard

Transportation accounts for forty percent of California's annual greenhouse gas emissions, and California relies on petroleum-based fuels for 96 percent of its transportation needs.

The Californian Governor Arnold Schwarzenegger announced an Executive Order that California adopt so-called Low Carbon Fuel Standard (LCFS). The LCFS requires fuel providers to ensure that the mix of fuel they sell in the California Market meets, on average, a declining target for greenhouse gas emissions measured in CO_2-equivalent grammes per unit of fuel energy sold. By 2020, the LCFS will produce a 10% reduction in GHG emissions from production and use of fuel in passenger vehicles in California.

Americas

USA

In the United States, emissions standards are managed by the Environmental Protection Agency (EPA) as well as some state governments.

Some of the strictest standards in the world are enforced in California by the California Air Resources Board (CARB), following the 2002 enactment of California AB 1493, which includes regulation of greenhouse gases.

Light-duty Vehicles

Currently, vehicles sold in the United States must meet "Tier II" standards that went into effect in 2004. "Tier II" standards are currently being phased in-a process that should be complete by 2009. Within the Tier II ranking, there is a subranking ranging from BIN 1-10, with 1 being the cleanest (Zero Emission vehicle) and 10 being the dirtiest. The former Tier 1 standards that were effective from 1994 until 2003 were different between automobiles and light trucks (SUVs, pickup trucks, and minivans), but Tier II standards are the same for both types.

A common measurement system for American standards is the somewhat confusing mixed-standard unit of grams per mile.

There are several ratings that can be given to vehicles. A certain percentage of the cars produced by major manufacturers must meet these different levels in order for the company to sell their products in affected regions. Tier 1 has been the baseline used. Beyond Tier 1, in increasing stringency, there are:

- TLEV-Transitional Low Emission Vehicle
- LEV-Low Emission Vehicle
- ULEV-Ultra-Low Emission Vehicle
- SULEV-Super-Ultra Low Emission Vehicle
- ZEV-Zero Emission Vehicle

The last category is largely restricted to electric vehicles and hydrogen cars, although such vehicles are usually not entirely non-polluting. In those cases, the other emissions are transferred to another site, such as a power plant or hydrogen reforming center, unless such sites run on renewable energy. However, a battery-powered electric vehicle charged from the California power grid will still be up to ten times cleaner than even the cleanest gasoline vehicles over their respective lifetimes.

The above standards are being made even more stringent. Tier 2 variations are appended with "II", such as LEV II or

SULEV II. There are other categories that have also been created.

- ILEV-Inherently Low-Emission Vehicle
- PZEV-Partial Zero Emission Vehicle
- AT-PZEV-Advanced Technology Partial Zero Emission Vehicle
- NLEV-National Low Emission Vehicle

PZEVs meet SULEV emission standards, but in addition have zero evaporative emissions and an extended (15-year/ 150,000 mile) warranty on their emission-control equipment. Several ordinary gasoline vehicles from the 2001 and later model years qualify as PZEVs; in addition, if a PZEV has technology that can also be used in ZEVs like an electric motor or high-pressure gaseous fuel tanks for compressed natural gas (CNG) or liquified petroleum gas (LPG), it qualifies as an AT-PZEV. Hybrid electric vehicles like the Toyota Prius can qualify, as can internal combustion engine vehicles that run on natural gas like the Honda Civic GX. These vehicles are called "partial" ZEVs because they receive partial credit in place of ZEVs that automakers would otherwise be required to sell in California.

The Greenhouse Gas Score reflects the exhaust emissions of carbon dioxide (CO_2), a greenhouse gas, and one of the biggest by-products of engine combustion. The Greenhouse Gas Score allows you to compare the expected amount of greenhouse gas emissions for different vehicles. The scoring is from 0 to 10, where 10 is the best because it represents the lowest amount of greenhouse gases.

"In Europe and the United States, particulate emissions from vehicles are expected to decline over the next decade. For example, by 2005, the European Union will introduce more stringent standards for particulate emissions from light duty vehicles of 0.025 grams per kilometer [0.04 grams per mile]. Even under these standards, diesel-powered cars may still warm the climate more over the next 100 years than may gasoline-powered cars, according to the study.

The state of California is implementing an even more restrictive standard in 2004, allowing only 0.006 grams per kilometer [0.01 grams per mile] of particulate emissions. Even if the California standard were introduced worldwide, says Jacobson, diesel cars may still warm the climate more than gasoline cars over 13 to 54 years." Particulate Emissions

California standard uses grams per mile average CO_2-equivalent value, which means that emissions of the various greenhouse gases are weighted to take into account their differing impact on climate change (i.e. in 2009, 323 g/mi for passenger cars).

Heavy-duty Vehicles

The European Union has its own set of emission standards that all new vehicles must meet. Currently, standards are set for all road vehicles, trains, barges and 'nonroad mobile machinery' (such as tractors). No standards apply to seagoing ships or airplanes. The emissions standards change based on the test cycle used: ECE R49 (old) and ESC (European Steady Cycle, since 2000).

Currently there are no standards for CO2 emissions. The European Parliament has suggested to introduce mandatory CO_2 emission standards to replace current voluntary commitments by the automanufacturers (see ACEA agreement) and labelling. In late 2005, the European Commission started working on a proposal for a new law to limit CO_2 emissions from cars. Sigmar Gabriel, Germany's environment minister, rebuffs calls to extend deadline to implement CO_2 reduction standards.

Transport and Environment (T&E) said new-car emissions from European producers slipped to 160 grams per kilometre (g/km) on average last year (0.2 percent in 2006), still way off a voluntary goal of 140 g/km by 2008.

Due to rapidly expanding wealth and prosperity, the number of coal power plants and cars on China's roads is rapidly growing, creating an ongoing pollution problem. China enacted its first emissions controls on automobiles in 2000, equivalent to Euro I standards.

They were upgraded again in 2005 to Euro II. More stringent emission standard, National Standard III, equivalent to Euro III standards went into effect on July 1st 2007.

Plans are for Euro IV standards to take effect in 2010. Beijing introduced the Euro IV standard in advance on January 1st 2008, became the first China's mainland city which adopted this standard.

Hong Kong

Hong Kong emission standards are totally independent from regulation of China.

From Jan 1, 2006, all new passenger cars in Hong Kong must meet Euro IV petrol standard.

India

The first Indian emission regulations were idle emission limits which became effective in 1989. These idle emission regulations were soon replaced by mass emission limits for both gasoline (1991) and diesel (1992) vehicles, which were gradually tightened during the 1990's. Since the year 2000, India started adopting European emission and fuel regulations for four-wheeled light-duty and for heavy-dc. Indian own emission regulations still apply to two-and three-wheeled vehicles.

On October 6, 2003, the National Auto Fuel Policy has been announced, which envisages a phased program for introducing Euro 2-4 emission and fuel regulations by 2010. The implementation schedule of EU emission standards in India is summarized in Table below.

Table: Indian Emission Standards (4-Wheel Vehicles)

Standard	Reference	Date	Region
India 2000	Euro 1	2000	Nationwide
Bharat Stage II	Euro 2	2001	NCR*, Mumbai, Kolkata, Chennai
		2003.04	NCR*, 10 Cities†
		2005.04	Nationwide
Bharat Stage III	Euro 3	2005.04	NCR*, 10 Cities†
		2010.04	Nationwide
Bharat Stage IV	Euro 4	2010.04	NCR*, 10 Cities†

* National Capital Region (Delhi)

† Mumbai, Kolkata, Chennai, Bangalore, Hyderabad, Ahmedabad, Pune, Surat, Kanpur and Agra

The above standards apply to all new 4-wheel vehicles sold and registered in the respective regions. In addition, the National Auto Fuel Policy introduces certain emission requirements for interstate buses with routes originating or terminating in Delhi or the other 10 cities.

For 2-and 3-wheelers, Bharat Stage II (Euro 2) will be applicable from April 1, 2005 and Stage III (Euro 3) standards would come in force preferably from April 1, 2008, but not later than April 1, 2010.

Trucks and Buses

Emission standards for new heavy-duty diesel engines-applicable to vehicles of GVW > 3,500 kg-are listed in Table 1. Emissions are tested over the ECE R49 13-mode test (through the Euro II stage)

Table: Emission Standards for Diesel Truck and Bus Engines, g/kWh

Year	Reference	CO	HC	NOx	PM
1992	-	17.3-32.6	2.7-3.7	-	-
1996	-	11.20	2.40	14.4	-
2000	Euro I	4.5	1.1	8.0	0.36*
2005†	Euro II	4.0	1.1	7.0	0.15
2010†	Euro III	2.1	0.66	5.0	0.10

* 0.612 for engines below 85 kW

† earlier introduction in selected regions.

More details on Euro I-III regulations can be found in the EU heavy-duty engine standards page.

Light Duty Diesel Vehicles

Emission standards for light-duty diesel vehicles (GVW = 3,500 kg) are summarized in Table below. Ranges of emission limits refer to different classes (by reference mass) of light commercial vehicles; compare the EU light-duty vehicle emission standards page for details on the Euro 1 and later standards. The lowest limit in each range applies to passenger cars (GVW = 2,500 kg; up to 6 seats).

Table: Emission Standards for Light-Duty Diesel Vehicles, g/km

Year	Reference	CO	HC	HC+NOx	PM
1992	-	17.3-32.6	2.7-3.7	-	-
1996	-	5.0-9.0	-	2.0-4.0	-
2000	Euro 1	2.72-6.90	-	0.97-1.70	0.14-0.25
2005†	Euro 2	1.0-1.5	-	0.7-1.2	0.08-0.17

† earlier introduction in selected regions

The test cycle has been the ECE + EUDC for low power vehicles (with maximum speed limited to 90 km/h). Before 2000, emissions were measured over an Indian test cycle.

Engines for use in light-duty vehicles can be also emission tested using an engine dynamometer. The respective emission standards are listed in Table below.

Table: Emission Standards for Light-Duty Diesel Engines, g/kWh

Year	Reference	CO	HC	NOx	PM
1992	-	14.0	3.5	18.0	-
1996	-	11.20	2.40	14.4	-
2000	Euro I	4.5	1.1	8.0	0.36*
2005†	Euro II	4.0	1.1	7.0	0.15

* 0.612 for engines below 85 kW

† earlier introduction in selected regions.

Light Duty Gasoline Vehicles

4-wheel Vehicles

Emission standards for gasoline vehicles (GVW = 3,500 kg) are summarized in Table 5. Ranges of emission limits refer to different classes of light commercial vehicles (compare the EU light-duty vehicle emission standards page). The lowest limit in each range applies to passenger cars (GVW = 2,500 kg; up to 6 seats).

Table: Emission Standards for Gasoline Vehicles (GVW = 3,500 kg), g/km

Year	Reference	CO	HC	HC+NOx
1991	-	14.3-27.1	2.0-2.9	-
1996	-	8.68-12.4	-	3.00-4.36
1998*	-	4.34-6.20	-	1.50-2.18
2000	Euro 1	2.72-6.90	-	0.97-1.70
2005†	Euro 2	2.2-5.0	-	0.5-0.7

* for catalytic converter fitted vehicles

† earlier introduction in selected regions, see Table 1

Gasoline vehicles must also meet an evaporative (SHED) limit of 2 g/test (effective 2000).

3-and 2-wheel Vehicles

Emission standards for 3-and 2-wheel gasoline vehicles are listed in the following tables.

Table: Emission Standards for 3-Wheel Gasoline Vehicles, g/km

Year	CO	HC	HC+NOx
1991	12-30	8-12	-
1996	6.75	-	5.40
2000	4.00	-	2.00
2005 (BS II)	2.25	-	2.00

Table: Emission Standards for 2-Wheel Gasoline Vehicles, g/km

Year	CO	HC	HC+NOx
1991	12-30	8-12	-
1996	5.50	-	3.60
2000	5.00	-	2.00
2005 (BS II)	1.50	-	1.50

Overview of the Emission Norms in India

- 1991-Idle CO Limits for Gasoline Vehicles and Free Acceleration Smoke for Diesel Vehicles, Mass Emission Norms for Gasoline Vehicles.
- 1992-Mass Emission Norms for Diesel Vehicles.
- 1996-Revision of Mass Emission Norms for Gasoline and Diesel Vehicles, mandatory fitment of Catalytic Converter for Cars in Metros on Unleaded Gasoline.
- 1998-Cold Start Norms Introduced.

- 2000-India 2000 (Eq. to Euro I) Norms, Modified IDC (Indian Driving Cycle), Bharat Stage II Norms for Delhi.
- 2001-Bharat Stage II (Eq. to Euro II) Norms for All Metros, Emission Norms for CNG & LPG Vehicles.
- 2003-Bharat Stage II (Eq. to Euro II) Norms for 11 major cities.
- 2005-From 1st April Bharat Stage III (Eq. to Euro III) Norms for 11 major cities.
- 2010-Bharat Stage III Emission Norms for 4-wheelers for entire country whereas Bharat Stage-IV (Eq. to Euro IV) for 11 major cities.

Japan

In 1992, to cope with NOx pollution problems from existing vehicle fleets in highly populated metropolitan areas, the Ministry of the Environment adopted the "Law Concerning Special Measures to Reduce the Total Amount of Nitrogen Oxides Emitted from Motor Vehicles in Specified Areas", called in short The Motor Vehicle NOx Law.

The regulation designated a total of 196 communities in the Tokyo, Saitama, Kanagawa, Osaka and Hyogo Prefectures as areas with significant air pollution due to nitrogen oxides emitted from motor vehicles. Under the Law, several measures had to be taken to control NOx from in-use vehicles, including enforcing emission standards for specified vehicle categories.

The regulation was amended in June 2001 to tighten the existing NOx requirements and to add PM control provisions. The amended rule is called the "Law Concerning Special Measures to Reduce the Total Amount of Nitrogen Oxides and Particulate Matter Emitted from Motor Vehicles in Specified Areas", or in short the Automotive NOx and PM Law.

The amended regulation became effective starting in October 2002. Emission Standards.

The NOx and PM Law introduces emission standards for specified categories of in-use highway vehicles including commercial goods (cargo) vehicles such as trucks and vans, buses, and special purpose motor vehicles, irrespective of the fuel type. The regulation also applies to diesel powered passenger cars (but not to gasoline cars).

In-use vehicles in the specified categories must meet 1997/98 emission standards for the respective new vehicle type (in the case of heavy duty engines NOx = 4.5 g/kWh, PM = 0.25 g/kWh). In other words, the 1997/98 new vehicle standards are retroactively applied to older vehicles already on the road. Vehicle owners have two methods to comply:

1. Replace old vehicles with newer, cleaner models

2. Retrofit old vehicles with approved NOx and PM control devices

Vehicles have a grace period, between 9 and 12 years from the initial registration, to comply. The grace period depends on the vehicle type, as follows:

* Light commercial vehicles (GVW = 2500 kg): 8 years

* Heavy commercial vehicles (GVW > 2500 kg): 9 years

* Micro buses (11-29 seats): 10 years

* Large buses (= 30 seats): 12 years

* Special vehicles (based on a cargo truck or bus): 10 years

* Diesel passenger cars: 9 years

Furthermore, the regulation allows to postpone its requirements by an additional 0.5-2.5 years, depending on the age of the vehicle. This delay was introduced in part to harmonize the NOx and PM Law with the Tokyo diesel retrofit program. The NOx and PM Law is enforced in connection with Japanese vehicle inspection program, where non-complying vehicles cannot undergo the inspection in the designated areas. This, in turn, may trigger an injunction on the vehicle operation under the Road Transport Vehicle Law.

ROADWAY AIR DISPERSION MODELING

Roadway air dispersion modeling is the study of air pollutant transport from a roadway or other linear emitter. Computer models are required to conduct this analysis, because of the complex variables involved, including vehicle emissions, vehicle speed, meteorology, and terrain geometry. Line source dispersion has been studied since at least the 1960s, when the regulatory framework in the United States began requiring quantitative analysis of the air pollution consequences of major roadway and airport projects. By the early 1970s this subset of atmospheric dispersion models were being applied to real world cases of highway planning, even including some controversial court cases.

How the Model Works

The basic concept of the roadway air dispersion model is to calculate air pollutant levels in the vicinity of a highway or arterial roadway by considering them as line sources. The model takes into account source characteristics such as traffic volume, vehicle speeds, truck mix, and fleet emission controls; in addition, the roadway geometry, surrounding terrain and local meteorology are addressed. For example, many air quality standards require that certain near worst case meteorological conditions be applied.

The calculations are sufficiently complex that a computer model is essential to arrive at authoritative results, although workbook type manuals have been developed as screening techniques. In some cases where results must be refereed (such as legal cases), model validation may be needed with field test data in the local setting; this step is not usually warranted, because the best models have been extensively validated over a wide spectrum of input data variables.

The product of the calculations is usually a set of isopleths (air pollution contour maps), either in plan view or cross sectional view. Typically these might be stated as concentrations of carbon monoxide, total reactive hydrocarbons, oxides of nitrogen, particulate or benzene. The air quality scientist can run the model successively to study techniques of reducing adverse air pollutant concentrations (for example, by redesigning roadway geometry, altering speed controls or limiting certain types of trucks). The model is frequently utilized in an Environmental Impact Statement involving a major new roadway or land use change which will induce new vehicular traffic.

History

The logical building block for this theory was the use of the Gaussian air pollutant dispersion equation for point sources. One of the early point source air pollutant plume dispersion equations was derived by Bosanquet and Pearson in 1936. Their equation did not include the effect of ground reflection of the pollutant plume. Sir Graham Sutton derived a point source air pollutant plume dispersion equation in 1947 which included the assumption of Gaussian distribution for the vertical and crosswind dispersion of the plume and also addressed the effect of ground reflection of the plume. Further advances were made by G. A. Briggs in model refinement and validation and by D.B. Turner for his user-friendly workbook that included screening calculations which do not require a computer.

In seeing the need to develop a line source model to approach the study of roadway air pollution, Michael Hogan and Richard Venti developed a closed form solution to integrating the point source equation in a series of publications.

While the ESL mathematical model was completed for a line source by 1970, model refinement resulted in a "strip source", emulating the horizontal extent of the roadway surface. This theory would be the precursor of area source dispersion models. But their focus was roadway simulation, so they proceeded with the development of a computer model by adding to the team Leda Patmore, a computer programmer in the field of atmospheric physics and satellite trajectory calculations. A working computer model was produced by late 1970; then the model was calibrated with carbon monoxide field measurements targeting from traffic on U.S. Route 101 in Sunnyvale, California.

The ESL model received endorsement from the U.S. Environmental Protection Agency (EPA) in the form of a major grant to validate the model using actual roadway tests of tracer gas sulfur hexafluoride dispersion. That gas was chosen since it does not occur naturally or in vehicular emissions and provides a unique tracer for such dispersion studies. Part of the Environmental Protection Agency's motives may have been to bring the model into public domain. After a successful validation through the EPA research, the model was soon put to use in a variety of settings to forecast air pollution levels in the vicinity of roadways. The ESL group applied the model to the U.S. Route 101 bypass project in Cloverdale, California, the extension of Interstate 66 through Arlington, Virginia, the widening of the New Jersey Turnpike through Raritan and East Brunswick, New Jersey, and several transportation projects in Boston for the Boston Transportation Planning Review.

By the early 1970s at least two other research groups were known to be actively developing some type to roadway air dispersion model: the Environmental Research and Technology group of Lexington, Massachusetts and Caltrans headquarters in Sacramento, California. The Caline model of Caltrans borrowed some of the technology from the ESL Inc. group, since Caltrans funded some of the early model application work in Cloverdale and other locations and was given rights to use parts of their model.

Example Applications of the Model

There were several early applications of the model in somewhat dramatic cases. In 1971 the Arlington Coalition on Transportation (ACT) was the plaintiff in an action against the Virginia Highway Commission over the extension of Interstate 66 through Arlington, Virginia, having filed a suit in the U.S. District Court. The ESL model was used to produce calculations of air quality in the vicinity of the proposed highway. ACT won this case after a decision by the U.S. Fourth Circuit Court of Appeals. The court paid special attention to the plaintiff's expert calculations and testimony projecting that air quality levels would violate Federal ambient air quality standards as set forth in the Clean Air Act.

A second contentious case took place in East Brunswick, New Jersey where the New Jersey Turnpike Authority planned a major widening of the Turnpike. Again the roadway air dispersion model was employed to predict levels of air pollution for residences, schools and parks near the Turnpike. After an initial hearing in Superior Court where the ESL model results were set forth, the judge ordered the Turnpike Authority to negotiate with the plaintiff, Concerned Citizens of East Brunswick and develop air quality mitigation for the adverse effects. The Turnpike Authority hired ERT as its expert, and the two research teams negotiated a settlement to this case using the newly created roadway air dispersion models.

More Recent Model Refinements

The CALINE3 model is a steady-state Gaussian dispersion model designed to determine air pollution concentrations at receptor locations downwind of highways located in relatively uncomplicated terrain. CALINE3 is incorporated into the more elaborate CAL3QHC and CAL3QHCR models. CALINE3 is in widespread use due to its user friendly nature and promotion in governmental circles, but it falls short of analyzing the complexity of cases addressed by the original Hogan-Venti model. CAL3QHC and CAL3QHCR models are available in fortran programming language and are limited to carbon monoxide: they do, however, include an embedded traffic model to better assess dynamic features such as stalling traffic.

In addition, several more recent models have been developed that employ non-steady state Lagrangian puff algorithms. The HYROAD dispersion model has been developed through the National Cooperative Highway Research Program's Project 25-06, incorporating ROADWAY-2 model puff and steady-state plume algorithms (Rao et al., 2002).

The TRAQSIM model, developed as part of a Ph.D dissertation with support by the U.S. Department of Transportation's Volpe National Transportation Systems Center's Air Quality Facility is currently under the care of Wyle Laboratories. The model incorporates dynamic vehicle behavior with a non-steady state Gaussian puff algorithm. Unlike HYROAD, TRAQSIM combines traffic simulation, second-by-second modal emissions, and Gaussian puff dispersion into a fully integrated system (a true simulation) that models individual vehicles as discrete moving sources. TRAQSIM was developed as a next generation model to be the successor to the current CALINE3 and CAL3QHC regulatory models. The next step in the development of

TRAQSIM is to incorporate methods to model the dispersion of particulate matter (PM) and hazardous air pollutants (HAPs).

Several models have been developed that handle complex urban meteorology resulting from urban canyons. Examples include the Turner-Fairbank Highway Research Center'sCanyon Plume Box model, now in version 3 (CPB-3), the National Environmental Research Institute of Denmark's Operational Street Pollution Model (OSPM), and the MICRO-CALGRID model, which includes photochemistry, allowing for both primary and secondary species to be modeled.

Recent Applications in Legal Cases

Recent health literature indicating that residents near major roads face elevated rates of several adverse health outcomes has prompted legal dispute over the responsibility of transportation agencies to use roadway air dispersion models to characterize the impacts of new and expanded roadways, bus terminals, truck stops, and other sources.

Recently, the Sierra Club of Nevada sued the Nevada Department of Transportation and the Federal Highway Administration over its their failure to assess the impact of the expansion of US-95 in Las Vegas on neighborhood air quality.[2] The Sierra Club asserted that a supplemental Environmental Impact Statement should be issued to address emissions of hazardous air pollutants and particulate matter from new motor vehicle traffic. The plaintiffs asserted that modeling tools were available, including the Environmental Protection Agency's MOBILE6.2 model, the CALINE3 dispersion model, and other relevant models. The defendants won in the U.S. District Court under Judge Philip Pro, who ruled that the transportation agencies had acted in a manner that was not "arbitrary and capricious," despite the agencies' technical arguments regarding the lack of available modeling tools being contradicted by a number of peer-reviewed studies published in scientific journals (e.g. Korenstein and Piazza, Journal of Environmental Health, 2002). On appeal to the 9th Federal Circuit Court, the court stayed new construction on the highway pending the court's final decision. The Sierra Club and the defendants settled out of court, setting up a research program on the air quality impacts of US-95 on nearby schools.

A number of other high-profile cases have prompted environmental groups to call for dispersion modeling to be used to assess the air quality impacts of new transportation projects on nearby communities, but to date state transportation agencies and the Federal Highways Administration has claimed that no tools are available, despite models and guidance available through EPA's Support Center for Regulatory Air Models (SCRAM).

Among the more contentious of cases the Detroit Intermodal Freight Terminal and Detroit River International Crossing (Michigan, USA), and the expansion of Interstate 70 East in Denver (Colorado, USA).

In all of these cases, community-based organizations have asserted that modeling tools are available, but transportation planning agencies have asserted that too much uncertainty exits in all of the steps. A major concern for community-based organizations has been transportation agencies' unwillingness to define the level of uncertainty that they are willing to tolerate in air quality analyses, how that compares to the Environmental Protection Agency's guideline on air quality models, which addresses uncertainty and accuracy in model use.

5

Pollutants and Sources of Indoor Air Pollution

- Asbestos
- Biological Pollutants
- Carbon Monoxide
- Formaldehyde/Pressed Wood Products
- Household Cleaning and Maintenance, Personal Care, or Hobbies
- Lead
- Nitrogen Dioxide
- Pesticides
- Radon
- Respirable Particles
- Secondhand Smoke/Environmental Tobacco Smoke
- Stoves, Heaters, Fireplaces, and Chimneys

PESTICIDES

According to a recent survey, 75 percent of U.S. households used at least one pesticide product indoors during the past year. Products used most often are insecticides and disinfectants. Another study suggests that 80 percent of most people's exposure to pesticides occurs indoors and that measurable levels of up to a dozen pesticides have been found in the air inside homes. The amount of pesticides found in homes appears to be greater than can be explained by recent pesticide use in those households; other possible sources include contaminated soil or dust that floats or is tracked in from outside, stored pesticide containers, and household surfaces that collect and then release the pesticides.

Pesticides used in and around the home include products to control insects (insecticides), termites (termiticides), rodents (rodenticides), fungi (fungicides), and microbes (disinfectants). They are sold as sprays, liquids, sticks, powders, crystals, balls, and foggers. In 1990, the American Association of Poison Control Centers reported that some 79,000 children were involved in common household pesticide poisonings or exposures. In households with children under five years old, almost one-half stored at least one pesticide product within reach of children.

EPA registers pesticides for use and requires manufacturers to put information on the label about when and how to use the pesticide. It is important to remember that the "-cide" in pesticides means "to kill". These products can be dangerous if not used properly. In addition to the active ingredient, pesticides are also made up of ingredients that are used to carry the active agent. These carrier agents are called "inerts" in pesticides because they are not toxic to the targeted pest; nevertheless, some inerts are capable of causing health problems.

Sources of Pesticides

Products used to kill household pests (insecticides, termiticides, and disinfectants). Also, products used on lawns and gardens that drift or are tracked inside the house. Pesticides are classed as semi-volatile organic compounds and include a variety of chemicals in various forms. Pesticides are chemicals that are used to kill or control pests which include bacteria, fungi, and other organisms, in addition to insects and rodents. Pesticides are inherently toxic.

HEALTH EFFECTS

Irritation to eye, nose, and throat; damage to central nervous system and kidney; increased risk of cancer. Symptoms may include headache, dizziness, muscular weakness, and nausea. Chronic exposure to some pesticides can result in damage to the liver, kidneys, endocrine and nervous systems. Both the active and inert ingredients in pesticides can be organic compounds; therefore, both could add to the levels of airborne organics inside homes. Both types of ingredients can cause the type of effects discussed in Household Chemicals/Products.

However, as with other household products, there is insufficient understanding at present about what pesticide concentrations are necessary to produce these effects. Exposure to high levels of cyclodiene pesticides, commonly associated with misapplication, has produced various symptoms, including headaches, dizziness, muscle twitching, weakness, tingling sensations, and nausea.

In addition, EPA is concerned that cyclodienes might cause long-term damage to the liver and the central nervous system, as well as an increased risk of cancer. There is no further sale or commercial use permitted for the following cyclodiene or related pesticides: chlordane, aldrin, dieldrin, and heptachlor. The only exception is the use of heptachlor by utility companies to control fire ants in underground cable boxes.

LEVELS IN HOMES

Preliminary research shows widespread presence of pesticide residues in homes.

Steps to Reduce Exposure:

- Use strictly according to manufacturer's directions.
- Mix or dilute outdoors.

- Apply only in recommended quantities.
- Increase ventilation when using indoors. Take plants or pets outdoors when applying pesticides/flea and tick treatments.
- Use non-chemical methods of pest control where possible.
- If you use a pest control company, select it carefully.
- Do not store unneeded pesticides inside home; dispose of unwanted containers safely.
- Store clothes with moth repellents in separately ventilated areas, if possible.
- Keep indoor spaces clean, dry, and well ventilated to avoid pest and odor problems.

Read the label and follow the directions. It is illegal to use any pesticide in any manner inconsistent with the directions on its label. Unless you have had special training and are certified, never use a pesticide that is restricted to use by state-certified pest control operators. Such pesticides are simply too dangerous for application by a non-certified person. Use only the pesticides approved for use by the general public and then only in recommended amounts; increasing the amount does not offer more protection against pests and can be harmful to you and your plants and pets.

Ventilate the Area well After Pesticide Use

Mix or dilute pesticides outdoors or in a well-ventilated area and only in the amounts that will be immediately needed. If possible, take plants and pets outside when applying pesticides/flea and tick treatments.

Use Non-chemical Methods of Pest Control when Possible

Since pesticides can be found far from the site of their original application, it is prudent to reduce the use of chemical pesticides outdoors as well as indoors. Depending on the site and pest to be controlled, one or more of the following steps can be effective: use of biological pesticides, such as Bacillus thuringiensis, for the control of gypsy moths; selection of disease-resistant plants; and frequent washing of indoor plants and pets. Termite damage can be reduced or prevented by making certain that wooden building materials do not come into direct contact with the soil and by storing firewood away from the home. By appropriately fertilizing, watering, and aerating lawns, the need for chemical pesticide treatments of lawns can be dramatically reduced.

If you decide to use a pest control company, choose one carefully. Ask for an inspection of your home and get a written control program for evaluation before you sign a contract. The control program should list specific names of pests to be controlled and chemicals to be used; it should also reflect any of your safety concerns. Insist on a proven record of competence and customer satisfaction.

Dispose of Unwanted Pesticides Safely

If you have unused or partially used pesticide containers you want to get rid of, dispose of them according to the directions on the label or on special household hazardous waste collection days. If there are no such collection days in your community, work with others to organize them.

Keep Exposure to Moth Repellents to a Minimum

One pesticide often found in the home is paradichlorobenzene, a commonly used active ingredient in moth repellents. This chemical is known to cause cancer in animals, but substantial scientific uncertainty exists over the effects, if any, of long-term human exposure to paradichlorobenzene. EPA requires that products containing paradichlorobenzene bear warnings such as "avoid breathing vapors" to warn users of potential short-term toxic effects.

Where possible, paradichlorobenzene, and items to be protected against moths, should be placed in trunks or other containers that can be stored in areas that are separately ventilated from the home, such as attics and detached garages. Paradichlorobenzene is also the key active ingredient in many air fresheners (in fact, some labels for moth repellents recommend that these same products be used as air fresheners or deodorants). Proper ventilation and basic household cleanliness will go a long way toward preventing unpleasant odors.

Outdoor Air Quality

- Pollutants
- Monitoring
- Transportation
- Smog
- Point sources
- Climate change
- Cosmetic pesticides
- Heating
- Open burning

Cosmetic Pesticides

Cosmetic pesticides can hurt the environment and human health. There is good news for people who want to keep their lawn and garden pretty : there are many healthy and safe alternatives to harmful cosmetic pesticides.

What are Cosmetic Pesticides?

Cosmetic pesticides are chemical or biological substances used to destroy living things such as: insects (insecticides), plants (herbicides), and fungi (fungicides) for the purpose of enhancing the appearance of a lawn or garden. They are sold commonly as sprays, liquids, powders or combined with chemical fertilizers.

How do Pesticides get into our Bodies?

Cosmetic pesticides can enter our bodies through skin contact, by ingestion (swallowing them, eg. on home-grown vegetables) or by breathing them in (inhalation). Pesticides can enter your home in a variety of ways:

- through people and pets
- through objects and toys contaminated with the chemicals
- through storage

There is always some drift with spraying of lawn and garden pesticides. Many pesticides linger after they've been applied.

How can Cosmetic Pesticides Hurt Human Health?

In the short term, cosmetic pesticides can be a problem for people who have multiple chemical sensitivities, or people who have lung diseases. They can set off an immediate physical reaction, such as an asthma attack. In the long term, pesticides are a concern. They cannot be properly tested for long-term adverse health effects on humans from foetal stage to old age. The mix of chemicals to which we are exposed or the varied responses of humans can't be replicated under laboratory conditions. It stands to reason that if pesticides can kill living things, then pesticides may harm us.

Symptoms of Pesticide Exposure

Pesticides are a broad category of complex chemicals, which may cause many immediate and long term negative health effects. These range from:

- mild symptoms such as headaches, fatigue and shortness of breath

- serious reactions like vomiting and loss of consciousness
- long term adverse effects on behaviour, and the nervous, immune and endocrine systems
- forms of cancer, such as non-Hodgkins lymphoma, leukemia and soft tissue sarcoma.

Use better gardening techniques, so you won't need pesticides. The best way to avoid air pollution from cosmetic pesticides is to not use them at all. The alternative is to implement an integrated pest-management program that promotes healthy plants:

Promote Healthy Soil

- Get your soil's pH and mineral content tested by collecting about 1/4 cup of soil from ten spots around the lawn, mixing it all together, and taking the sample it to your provincial Department of Agriculture for testing.
- Use lime to increase your soil's pH for plants like turf grasses that are vulnerable in acidic soil.
- Use organic fertilizer (such as compost) to increase the nutrients available to plants, to improve soil structure and water-holding capacity, and to encourage earthworm and microorganism populations. Chemical fertilizer only provides nutrients and can get washed into groundwater, becoming a source of nitrate contamination.
- Hire a lawn-care company, rent an aerator or use a garden rake to aerate your compacted lawn soil. A healthy population of earthworms provides this service over the long term.
- For healthy lawn turf, mow high (3"), mow often, and leave the clippings, which will provide at least one third of the nitrogen requirements of the grass.

- Add a low-growing clover to your lawn to provide nitrogen naturally through microorganisms that live on the roots and procure nitrogen from the air.

Increase Biodiversity

- Trees, shrubs, and a variety of plant species attract a diversity of birds and insects to act as natural controls on each other, so that no one species gets out of balance. Native plant species are the best adapted to local conditions.
- Try substituting alternative ground covers such as creeping or wooly thyme, spreading junipers, creeping jenny, mosses, ferns and wild flowers for lawns.
- Add perennial beds to create a garden, rather than a having a large expansive lawn.
- Rethink what constitutes a weed on your lawn. Besides providing nitrogen, clover stays green in the dry heat of midsummer. Assorted lawn covers provide a variety of textures and colours, and discourage insect attacks from pests like white grubs or chinch bugs.

Ensure you Grow the Right Plants for your Location and Conditions

- Consult your local garden club or centre for advice on appropriate trees, shrubs, plants, and turf grasses for your climate zone.
- Place plants according to whether they thrive in sun, shade, dry and/or wet areas.
- Choose plants native to your area.

If you do have a pest infestation: alternatives to chemical pesticides. If you do have an explosion of a particular pest population, use non-toxic or food grade products to remedy the situation. The following are a few simple, non-toxic solutions to combat various pests:

Pest	Control Method	Source
Dandelions	• Treat with boiling vinegar • Hand weed in moist soil	
Pre-emergent Dandelions (before they emerge from the ground)	• Corn gluten	Available at some garden centres
Ants	• Sprinkle borax mixed with a bit of icing sugar on the hill • Pour boiling water over the hill • Sprinkle bone meal or cayenne pepper across ants' point of entry into the house	Borax can be found in the laundry section of the grocery store
Aphids	• Spray plants with 1Tbs of ordinary dish detergent in 4 litres of garlic water • Promote ladybugs through plant diversity • Plant nasturtiums, garlic, chives, or petunias beside vulnerable plants to repel aphids	Ladybugs are available commercially
Army Worms Tent Caterpillars	• Manually remove nests on trees in spring: use a pole or brush if they are located high in trees • Place tape covered with petroleum jelly around uninfected tree trunks	
Chinch Bug	• Place a wet old sheet or newspapers over the dead patch of grass • Chinch bugs will cling to the bottom	

Earwigs	• Trap them in rolls of damp newspaper	
Gypsy Moth	• Scrape tan, oval-shaped egg masses off hard surfaces in fall, winter or early spring • Wrap a couple of layers of burlap around a tree trunk and fold over the top. This will trap the pupating larvae towards the end of July.	
Slugs	• Slugs will drown in dishes of beer placed among plants • Trap slugs under boards placed in the garden	
Spiders on house	• Turn off some of the lights that attract flies which attract spiders	
White Grub (Japanese beetle larvae)	• Treat infected area with predatory nematodes • Walk over infected areas several times in shoes with long spikes on the soles (aerator sandals) • Plant geraniums to repel them • In the early morning, shake them off trees and shrubs onto a sheet	Nematodes and aerator sandals are available at some garden centres.

The Lung Association advises against the use of cosmetic pesticides.

If your neighbours are spraying, try educating them in collaboration with the local garden club or centre, by organizing community group, neighbourhood or workplace talks.

INDOOR AIR QUALITY CONCERNS

All of us face a variety of risks to our health as we go about our day-to-day lives. Driving in cars, flying in planes, engaging in recreational activities, and being exposed to environmental pollutants all pose varying degrees of risk. Some risks are simply unavoidable. Some we choose to accept because to do otherwise would restrict our ability to lead our lives the way we want. And some are risks we might decide to avoid if we had the opportunity to make informed choices. Indoor air pollution is one risk that you can do something about.

In the last several years, a growing body of scientific evidence has indicated that the air within homes and other buildings can be more seriously polluted than the outdoor air in even the largest and most industrialized cities. Other research indicates that people spend approximately 90 percent of their time indoors. Thus, for many people, the risks to health may be greater due to exposure to air pollution indoors than outdoors.

In addition, people who may be exposed to indoor air pollutants for the longest periods of time are often those most susceptible to the effects of indoor air pollution. Such groups include the young, the elderly, and the chronically ill, especially those suffering from respiratory or cardiovascular disease.

Why a Booklet on Indoor Air?

While pollutant levels from individual sources may not pose a significant health risk by themselves, most homes have more than one source that contributes to indoor air pollution. There can be a serious risk from the cumulative effects of these sources. Fortunately, there are steps that most people can take both to reduce the risk from existing sources and to prevent new problems from occurring. This booklet was prepared by the U.S. Environmental Protection Agency (EPA) and the U.S. Consumer Product Safety Commission (CPSC) to help you decide whether to take actions that can reduce the level of indoor air pollution in your own home.

Because so many Americans spend a lot of time in offices with mechanical heating, cooling, and ventilation systems, there is also a short section on the causes of poor air quality in offices and what you can do if you suspect that your office may have a problem. A glossary and a list of organizations where you can get additional information are available in this document.

INDOOR AIR QUALITY IN YOUR HOME

What Causes Indoor Air Problems?

Indoor pollution sources that release gases or particles into the air are the primary cause of indoor air quality problems in homes. Inadequate ventilation can increase indoor pollutant levels by not bringing in enough outdoor air to dilute emissions from indoor sources and by not carrying indoor air pollutants out of the home. High temperature and humidity levels can also increase concentrations of some pollutants.

Pollutant Sources

There are many sources of indoor air pollution in any home. These include combustion sources such as oil, gas, kerosene, coal, wood, and tobacco products; building materials and furnishings as diverse as deteriorated, asbestos-containing insulation, wet or damp carpet, and cabinetry or furniture made of certain pressed wood products; products for household cleaning and maintenance, personal care, or hobbies; central heating and cooling systems and humidification devices; and outdoor sources such as radon, pesticides, and outdoor air pollution.

The relative importance of any single source depends on how much of a given pollutant it emits and how hazardous those emissions are. In some cases, factors such as how old the source is and whether it is properly maintained are significant. For example, an improperly adjusted gas stove can emit significantly more carbon monoxide than one that is properly adjusted.

Some sources, such as building materials, furnishings, and household products like air fresheners, release pollutants more or less continuously. Other sources, related to activities carried out in the home, release pollutants intermittently. These include smoking, the use of unvented or malfunctioning stoves, furnaces, or space heaters, the use of solvents in cleaning and hobby activities, the use of paint strippers in redecorating activities, and the use of cleaning products and pesticides in housekeeping. High pollutant concentrations can remain in the air for long periods after some of these activities.

Amount of Ventilation

If too little outdoor air enters a home, pollutants can accumulate to levels that can pose health and comfort problems. Unless they are built with special mechanical means of ventilation, homes that are designed and constructed to minimize the amount of outdoor air that can "leak" into and out of the home may have higher pollutant levels than other homes. However, because some weather conditions can drastically reduce the amount of outdoor air that enters a home, pollutants can build up even in homes that are normally considered "leaky."

How Does Outdoor Air Enter a House?

Outdoor air enters and leaves a house by: infiltration, natural ventilation, and mechanical ventilation. In a process known as infiltration, outdoor air flows into the house through openings, joints, and cracks in walls, floors, and ceilings, and around windows and doors. In natural ventilation, air moves through opened windows and doors. Air movement associated with infiltration and natural ventilation is caused by air temperature differences between indoors and outdoors and by wind. Finally, there are a number of mechanical ventilation devices, from outdoor-vented fans that intermittently remove air from a single room, such as bathrooms and kitchen, to air handling systems that use fans and duct work to continuously remove indoor air and distribute filtered and conditioned outdoor air to strategic points throughout the house.

The rate at which outdoor air replaces indoor air is described as the air exchange rate. When there is little infiltration, natural ventilation, or mechanical ventilation, the air exchange rate is low and pollutant levels can increase.

What if You Live in an Apartment?

Apartments can have the same indoor air problems as single-family homes because many of the pollution sources, such as the interior building materials, furnishings, and household products, are similar. Indoor air problems similar to those in offices are caused by such sources as contaminated ventilation systems, improperly placed outdoor air intakes, or maintenance activities.

Solutions to air quality problems in apartments, as in homes and offices, involve such actions as: eliminating or controlling the sources of pollution, increasing ventilation, and installing air cleaning devices. Often a resident can take the appropriate action to improve the indoor air quality by removing a source, altering an activity, unblocking an air supply vent, or opening a window to temporarily increase the ventilation; in other cases, however, only the building owner or manager is in a position to remedy the problem.

Indoor Air and Your Health

Health effects from indoor air pollutants may be experienced soon after exposure or, possibly, years later.

Immediate effects may show up after a single exposure or repeated exposures. These include irritation of the eyes, nose, and throat, headaches, dizziness, and fatigue. Such immediate effects are usually short-term and treatable. Sometimes the treatment is simply eliminating the person's exposure to the source of the pollution, if it can be identified. Symptoms of some diseases, including asthma, hypersensitivity pneumonitis, and humidifier fever, may also show up soon after exposure to some indoor air pollutants.

The likelihood of immediate reactions to indoor air pollutants depends on several factors. Age and preexisting medical conditions are two important influences. In other cases, whether a person reacts to a pollutant depends on individual sensitivity, which varies tremendously from person to person. Some people can become sensitized to biological pollutants after repeated exposures, and it appears that some people can become sensitized to chemical pollutants as well.

Certain immediate effects are similar to those from colds or other viral diseases, so it is often difficult to determine if the symptoms are a result of exposure to indoor air pollution. For this reason, it is important to pay attention to the time and place the symptoms occur. If the symptoms fade or go away when a person is away from the home and return when the person returns, an effort should be made to identify indoor air sources that may be possible causes. Some effects may be made worse by an inadequate supply of outdoor air or from the heating, cooling, or humidity conditions prevalent in the home.

Other health effects may show up either years after exposure has occurred or only after long or repeated periods of exposure. These effects, which include some respiratory diseases, heart disease, and cancer, can be severely debilitating or fatal. It is prudent to try to improve the indoor air quality in your home even if symptoms are not noticeable. More information on potential health effects from particular indoor air pollutants is provided in the section, "A Look at Source-Specific Controls."

While pollutants commonly found in indoor air are responsible for many harmful effects, there is considerable uncertainty about what concentrations or periods of exposure are necessary to produce specific health problems. People also react very differently to exposure to indoor air pollutants. Further research is needed to better understand which health effects occur after exposure to the average pollutant concentrations found in homes and which occur from the higher concentrations that occur for short periods of time.

The health effects associated with some indoor air pollutants are summarized in the section "Reference Guide to Major Indoor Air Pollutants in the Home."

Identifying Air Quality Problems

Some health effects can be useful indicators of an indoor air quality problem, especially if they appear after a person moves to a new residence, remodels or refurnishes a home, or treats a home with pesticides. If you think that you have symptoms that may be related to your home environment, discuss them with your doctor or your local health department to see if they could be caused by indoor air pollution. You may also want to consult a board-certified allergist or an occupational medicine specialist for answers to your questions.

Another way to judge whether your home has or could develop indoor air problems is to identify potential sources of indoor air pollution. Although the presence of such sources does not necessarily mean that you have an indoor air quality problem, being aware of the type and number of potential sources is an important step toward assessing the air quality in your home.

A third way to decide whether your home may have poor indoor air quality is to look at your lifestyle and activities. Human activities can be significant sources of indoor air pollution. Finally, look for signs of problems with the ventilation in your home.

Signs that can indicate your home may not have enough ventilation include moisture condensation on windows or walls, smelly or stuffy air, dirty central heating and air cooling equipment, and areas where books, shoes, or other items become moldy. To detect odors in your home, step outside for a few minutes, and then upon reentering your home, note whether odors are noticeable.

Measuring Pollutant Levels

The federal government recommends that you measure the level of radon in your home. Without measurements there is no way to tell whether radon is present because it is a colorless, odorless, radioactive gas. Inexpensive devices are available for measuring radon. EPA provides guidance as to risks associated with different levels of exposure and when the public should consider corrective action. There are specific mitigation techniques that have proven effective in reducing levels of radon in the home.

For pollutants other than radon, measurements are most appropriate when there are either health symptoms or signs of poor ventilation and specific sources or pollutants have been identified as possible causes of indoor air quality problems. Testing for many pollutants can be expensive. Before monitoring your home for pollutants besides radon, consult your state or local health department or professionals who have experience in solving indoor air quality problems in nonindustrial buildings.

Weatherizing Your Home

The federal government recommends that homes be weatherized in order to reduce the amount of energy needed for heating and cooling. While weatherization is underway, however, steps should also be taken to minimize pollution from sources inside the home. In addition, residents should be alert to the emergence of signs of inadequate ventilation, such as stuffy air, moisture condensation on cold surfaces, or mold and mildew growth. Additional weatherization measures should not be undertaken until these problems have been corrected.

Weatherization generally does not cause indoor air problems by adding new pollutants to the air. (There are a few exceptions, such as caulking, that can sometimes emit pollutants.) However, measures such as installing storm windows, weather stripping, caulking, and blown-in wall insulation can reduce the amount of outdoor air infiltrating into a home. Consequently, after weatherization, concentrations of indoor air pollutants from sources inside the home can increase.

Three Basic Strategies

Source Control

Usually the most effective way to improve indoor air quality is to eliminate individual sources of pollution or to reduce their emissions.

Some sources, like those that contain asbestos, can be sealed or enclosed; others, like gas stoves, can be adjusted to decrease the amount of emissions. In many cases, source control is also a more cost-efficient approach to protecting indoor air quality than increasing ventilation because increasing ventilation can increase energy costs. Specific sources of indoor air pollution in your home are listed later in this section.

Ventilation Improvements

Another approach to lowering the concentrations of indoor air pollutants in your home is to increase the amount of outdoor air coming indoors. Most home heating and cooling systems, including forced air heating systems, do not mechanically bring fresh air into the house.

Opening windows and doors, operating window or attic fans, when the weather permits, or running a window air conditioner with the vent control open increases the outdoor ventilation rate. Local bathroom or kitchen fans that exhaust outdoors remove contaminants directly from the room where the fan is located and also increase the outdoor air ventilation rate.

It is particularly important to take as many of these steps as possible while you are involved in short-term activities that can generate high levels of pollutants--for example, painting, paint stripping, heating with kerosene heaters, cooking, or engaging in maintenance and hobby activities such as welding, soldering, or sanding. You might also choose to do some of these activities outdoors, if you can and if weather permits.

Advanced designs of new homes are starting to feature mechanical systems that bring outdoor air into the home. Some of these designs include energy-efficient heat recovery ventilators (also known as air-to-air heat exchangers).

Air Cleaners

There are many types and sizes of air cleaners on the market, ranging from relatively inexpensive table-top models to sophisticated and expensive whole-house systems. Some air cleaners are highly effective at particle removal, while others, including most table-top models, are much less so. Air cleaners are generally not designed to remove gaseous pollutants.

The effectiveness of an air cleaner depends on how well it collects pollutants from indoor air (expressed as a percentage efficiency rate) and how much air it draws through the cleaning or filtering element (expressed in cubic feet per minute). A very efficient collector with a low air-circulation rate will not be effective, nor will a cleaner with a high air-circulation rate but a less efficient collector. The long-term performance of any air cleaner depends on maintaining it according to the manufacturer's directions.

Another important factor in determining the effectiveness of an air cleaner is the strength of the pollutant source. Table-top air cleaners, in particular, may not remove satisfactory amounts of pollutants from strong nearby sources. People with a sensitivity to particular sources may find that air cleaners are helpful only in conjunction with concerted efforts to remove the source.

Over the past few years, there has been some publicity suggesting that houseplants have been shown to reduce levels of some chemicals in laboratory experiments. There is currently no evidence, however, that a reasonable number of houseplants remove significant quantities of pollutants in homes and offices. Indoor houseplants should not be over-watered because overly damp soil may promote the growth of microorganisms which can affect allergic individuals.

At present, EPA does not recommend using air cleaners to reduce levels of radon and its decay products. The effectiveness of these devices is uncertain because they only partially remove the radon decay products and do not diminish the amount of radon entering the home. EPA plans to do additional research on whether air cleaners are, or could become, a reliable means of reducing the health risk from radon. EPA's booklet, Residential Air-Cleaning Devices, provides further information on air-cleaning devices to reduce indoor air pollutants.

For most indoor air quality problems in the home, source control is the most effective solution. This section takes a source-by-source look at the most common indoor air pollutants, their potential health effects, and ways to reduce levels in the home. (For a summary of the points made in this section, see the section entitled "Reference Guide to Major Indoor Air Pollutants in the Home.") EPA has recently released, Ozone Generators That Are Sold As Air Cleaners. The purpose of this document is to provide accurate information regarding the use of ozone-generating devices in indoor occupied spaces. This information is based on the most credible scientific evidence currently available.

EPA has recently published, "Should You Have the Air Ducts in Your Home Cleaned?" This discussion is intended to help consumers answer this often confusing question. The document explains what air duct cleaning is, provides guidance to help consumers decide whether to have the service performed in their home, and provides helpful information for choosing a duct cleaner, determining if duct cleaning was done properly, and how to prevent contamination of air ducts.

A LOOK AT SOURCE-SPECIFIC CONTROLS RADON (RN)

The most common source of indoor radon is uranium in the soil or rock on which homes are built. As uranium naturally breaks down, it releases radon gas which is a colorless, odorless, radioactive gas. Radon gas enters homes through dirt floors, cracks in concrete walls and floors, floor drains, and sumps. When radon becomes trapped in buildings and concentrations build up indoors, exposure to radon becomes a concern.

Any home may have a radon problem. This means new and old homes, well-sealed and drafty homes, and homes with or without basements. Sometimes radon enters the home through well water. In a small number of homes, the building materials can give off radon, too. However, building materials rarely cause radon problems by themselves.

Health Effects of Radon

The predominant health effect associated with exposure to elevated levels of radon is lung cancer. Research suggests that swallowing water with high radon levels may pose risks, too, although these are believed to be much lower than those from breathing air containing radon. Major health organizations (like the Centers for Disease Control and Prevention, the American Lung Association (ALA), and the American Medical Association) agree with estimates that radon causes thousands of preventable lung cancer deaths each year. EPA estimates that radon causes about 14,000 deaths per year in the United States--however, this number could range from 7,000 to 30,000 deaths per year. If you smoke and your home has high radon levels, your risk of lung cancer is especially high.

Reducing Exposure to Radon in Homes

Measure levels of radon in your home.

You can't see radon, but it's not hard to find out if you have a radon problem in your home. Testing is easy and should only take a little of your time.

There are many kinds of inexpensive, do-it-yourself radon test kits you can get through the mail and in hardware stores and other retail outlets. Make sure you buy a test kit that has passed EPA's testing program or is state-certified. These kits will usually display the phrase "Meets EPA Requirements." If you prefer, or if you are buying or selling a home, you can hire a trained contractor to do the testing for you. EPA's voluntary National Radon Proficiency Program (RPP) evaluated testing (measurement) contractors. A contractor who had met EPA's requirements carried an EPA-generated RPP identification card. EPA provided a list of companies and individual contractors on this web site which was also available to state radon offices. You should call your state radon office to obtain a list of qualified contractors in your area.You can also contact either the National Environmental Health Association or the National Radon Safety Board (NRSB) for a list of proficient radon measurement and/or mitigation contractors.

Refer to the EPA guidelines on how to test and interpret your test results.

You can learn more about radon through EPA's publications, A Citizen's Guide to Radon: The Guide to Protecting Yourself and Your Family From Radon and Home Buyer's and Seller's Guide to Radon, which are also available from your state radon office.

Learn about Radon Reduction Methods

Ways to reduce radon in your home are discussed in EPA's Consumer's Guide to Radon Reduction. You can get a copy from your state radon office. There are simple solutions to radon problems in homes. Thousands of homeowners have already fixed radon problems. Lowering high radon levels requires technical knowledge and special skills. You should use a contractor who is trained to fix radon problems.

A trained radon reduction contractor can study the problem in your home and help you pick the correct treatment method. Check with your state radon office for names of qualified or state-certified radon-reduction contractors in your area.

Stop Smoking and Discourage Smoking in Your Home

Scientific evidence indicates that smoking combined with radon is an especially serious health risk. Stop smoking and lower your radon level to reduce lung cancer risk.

Treat Radon-contaminated Well Water

While radon in water is not a problem in homes served by most public water supplies, it has been found in well water. If you've tested the air in your home and found a radon problem, and you have a well, contact a lab certified to measure radiation in water to have your water tested. Radon problems in water can be readily fixed.

ENVIRONMENTAL TOBACCO SMOKE (ETS)

Environmental tobacco smoke (ETS) is the mixture of smoke that comes from the burning end of a cigarette, pipe, or cigar, and smoke exhaled by the smoker. It is a complex mixture of over 4,000 compounds, more than 40 of which are known to cause cancer in humans or animals and many of which are strong irritants. ETS is often referred to as "secondhand smoke" and exposure to ETS is often called "passive smoking."

Health Effects of Environmental Tobacco Smoke

In 1992, EPA completed a major assessment of the respiratory health risks of ETS. The report concludes that exposure to ETS is responsible for approximately 3,000 lung cancer deaths each year in nonsmoking adults and impairs the respiratory health of hundreds of thousands of children.

Infants and young children whose parents smoke in their presence are at increased risk of lower respiratory tract infections (pneumonia and bronchitis) and are more likely to have symptoms of respiratory irritation like cough, excess phlegm, and wheeze. EPA estimates that passive smoking annually causes between 150,000 and 300,000 lower respiratory tract infections in infants and children under 18 months of age, resulting in between 7,500 and 15,000 hospitalizations each year. These children may also have a build-up of fluid in the middle ear, which can lead to ear infections. Older children who have been exposed to secondhand smoke may have slightly reduced lung function.

Asthmatic children are especially at risk. EPA estimates that exposure to secondhand smoke increases the number of episodes and severity of symptoms in hundreds of thousands of asthmatic children, and may cause thousands of nonasth-matic children to develop the disease each year. EPA estimates that between 200,000 and 1,000,000 asthmatic children have their condition made worse by exposure to secondhand smoke each year. Exposure to secondhand smoke causes eye, nose, and throat irritation. It may affect the cardiovascular system and some studies have linked exposure to secondhand smoke with the onset of chest pain.

Reducing Exposure to Environmental Tobacco Smoke

Don't smoke at home or permit others to do so. Ask smokers to smoke outdoors.

The 1986 Surgeon General's report concluded that physical separation of smokers and nonsmokers in a common air space, such as different rooms within the same house, may reduce-but will not eliminate-non-smokers' exposure to environmental tobacco smoke.

If smoking indoors cannot be avoided, increase ventilation in the area where smoking takes place.

Open windows or use exhaust fans. Ventilation, a common method of reducing exposure to indoor air pollutants, also will reduce but not eliminate exposure to environmental tobacco smoke. Because smoking produces such large amounts of pollutants, natural or mechanical ventilation techniques do not remove them from the air in your home as quickly as they build up. In addition, the large increases in ventilation it takes to significantly reduce exposure to environmental tobacco smoke can also increase energy costs substantially. Consequently, the most effective way to reduce exposure to environmental tobacco smoke in the home is to eliminate smoking there.

Do not smoke if children are present, particularly infants and toddlers.

Children are particularly susceptible to the effects of passive smoking. Do not allow baby-sitters or others who work in your home to smoke indoors. Discourage others from smoking around children. Find out about the smoking policies of the day care center providers, schools, and other care givers for your children. The policy should protect children from exposure to ETS.

BIOLOGICAL CONTAMINANTS

Biological contaminants include bacteria, molds, mildew, viruses, animal dander and cat saliva, house dust mites, cockroaches, and pollen. There are many sources of these pollutants.

Pollens originate from plants; viruses are transmitted by people and animals; bacteria are carried by people, animals, and soil and plant debris; and household pets are sources of saliva and animal dander. The protein in urine from rats and mice is a potent allergen. When it dries, it can become airborne. Contaminated central air handling systems can become breeding grounds for mold, mildew, and other sources of biological contaminants and can then distribute these contaminants through the home.

By controlling the relative humidity level in a home, the growth of some sources of biologicals can be minimized. A relative humidity of 30-50 percent is generally recommended for homes. Standing water, water-damaged materials, or wet surfaces also serve as a breeding ground for molds, mildews, bacteria, and insects. House dust mites, the source of one of the most powerful biological allergens, grow in damp, warm environments.

Health Effects From Biological Contaminants

Some biological contaminants trigger allergic reactions, including hypersensitivity pneumonitis, allergic rhinitis, and some types of asthma. Infectious illnesses, such as influenza, measles, and chicken pox are transmitted through the air. Molds and mildews release disease-causing toxins. Symptoms of health problems caused by biological pollutants include sneezing, watery eyes, coughing, shortness of breath, dizziness, lethargy, fever, and digestive problems.

Allergic reactions occur only after repeated exposure to a specific biological allergen. However, that reaction may occur immediately upon re-exposure or after multiple exposures over time. As a result, people who have noticed only mild allergic reactions, or no reactions at all, may suddenly find themselves very sensitive to particular allergens.

Some diseases, like humidifier fever, are associated with exposure to toxins from microorganisms that can grow in large building ventilation systems. However, these diseases can also be traced to microorganisms that grow in home heating and cooling systems and humidifiers. Children, elderly people, and people with breathing problems, allergies, and lung diseases are particularly susceptible to disease-causing biological agents in the indoor air.

Reducing Exposure to Biological Contaminants

Install and use exhaust fans that are vented to the outdoors in kitchens and bathrooms and vent clothes dryers outdoors.

These actions can eliminate much of the moisture that builds up from everyday activities. There are exhaust fans on the market that produce little noise, an important consideration for some people. Another benefit to using kitchen and bathroom exhaust fans is that they can reduce levels of organic pollutants that vaporize from hot water used in showers and dishwashers.

Ventilate the attic and crawl spaces to prevent moisture build-up.

Keeping humidity levels in these areas below 50 percent can prevent water condensation on building materials.

If using cool mist or ultrasonic humidifiers, clean appliances according to manufacturer's instructions and refill with fresh water daily.

Because these humidifiers can become breeding grounds for biological contaminants, they have the potential for causing diseases such as hypersensitivity pneumonitis and humidifier fever. Evaporation trays in air conditioners, dehumidifiers, and refrigerators should also be cleaned frequently.

Thoroughly clean and dry water-damaged carpets and building materials (within 24 hours if possible) or consider removal and replacement.

Water-damaged carpets and building materials can harbor mold and bacteria. It is very difficult to completely rid such materials of biological contaminants.

Keep the house clean. House dust mites, pollens, animal dander, and other allergy-causing agents can be reduced, although not eliminated, through regular cleaning.

People who are allergic to these pollutants should use allergen-proof mattress encasements, wash bedding in hot (130 degrees farenheit) water, and avoid room furnishings that accumulate dust, especially if they cannot be washed in hot water. Allergic individuals should also leave the house while it is being vacuumed because vacuuming can actually increase airborne levels of mite allergens and other biological contaminants. Using central vacuum systems that are vented to the outdoors or vacuums with high efficiency filters may also be of help. Take steps to minimize biological pollutants in basements.

Clean and disinfect the basement floor drain regularly. Do not finish a basement below ground level unless all water leaks are patched and outdoor ventilation and adequate heat to prevent condensation are provided. Operate a dehumidifier in the basement if needed to keep relative humidity levels between 30-50 percent.

To learn more about biological pollutants, read Biological Pollutants in Your Home issued by the U.S. Consumer Product Safety Commission and the American Lung Association. For contact information, see the section, "Where to Go For Additional Information."

STOVES, HEATERS, FIREPLACES, AND CHIMNEYS

In addition to environmental tobacco smoke, other sources of combustion products are unvented kerosene and gas space heaters, woodstoves, fireplaces, and gas stoves. The major pollutants released are carbon monoxide, nitrogen dioxide, and particles. Unvented kerosene heaters may also generate acid aerosols.

Combustion gases and particles also come from chimneys and flues that are improperly installed or maintained and cracked furnace heat exchangers. Pollutants from fireplaces and woodstoves with no dedicated outdoor air supply can be "back-drafted" from the chimney into the living space, particularly in weatherized homes.

Health Effects of Combustion Products

Carbon monoxide (CO) is a colorless, odorless gas that interferes with the delivery of oxygen throughout the body. At high concentrations it can cause unconsciousness and death. Lower concentrations can cause a range of symptoms from headaches, d izziness, weakness, nausea, confusion, and disorientation, to fatigue in healthy people and episodes of increased chest pain in people with chronic heart disease. The symptoms of carbon monoxide poisoning are sometimes confused with the flu or food poisoning. Fetuses, infants, elderly people, and people with anemia or with a history of heart or respiratory disease can be especially sensitive to carbon monoxide exposures.

Nitrogen dioxide (NO2) is a colorless, odorless gas that irritates the mucous membranes in the eye, nose, and throat and causes shortness of breath after exposure to high concentrations. There is evidence that high concentrations or continued exposure to low levels of nitrogen dioxide increases the risk of respiratory infection; there is also evidence from animal studies that repeated exposures to elevated nitrogen dioxide levels may lead, or contribute, to the development of lung disease such as emphysema. People at particular risk from exposure to nitrogen dioxide include children and individuals with asthma and other respiratory diseases.

Particles, released when fuels are incompletely burned, can lodge in the lungs and irritate or damage lung tissue. A number of pollutants, including radon and benzo(a)pyrene, both of which can cause cancer, attach to small particles that are inhaled and then carried deep into the lung.

Reducing Exposure to Combustion Products in Homes

Take special precautions when operating fuel-burning unvented space heaters.

Consider potential effects of indoor air pollution if you use an unvented kerosene or gas space heater. Follow the manufacturer's directions, especially instructions on the proper fuel and keeping the heater properly adjusted. A persistent yellow-tipped flame is generally an indicator of maladjustment and increased pollutant emissions. While a space heater is in use, open a door from the room where the heater is located to the rest of the house and open a window slightly.

Install and use exhaust fans over gas cooking stoves and ranges and keep the burners properly adjusted.

Using a stove hood with a fan vented to the outdoors greatly reduces exposure to pollutants during cooking. Improper adjustment, often indicated by a persistent yellow-tipped flame, causes increased pollutant emissions. Ask your gas company to adjust the burner so that the flame tip is blue. If you purchase a new gas stove or range, consider buying one with pilotless ignition because it does not have a pilot light that burns continuously. Never use a gas stove to heat your home. Always make certain the flue in your gas fireplace is open when the fireplace is in use.

Keep woodstove emissions to a minimum. Choose properly sized new stoves that are certified as meeting EPA emission standards.

Make certain that doors in old woodstoves are tight-fitting. Use aged or cured (dried) wood only and follow the manufacturer's directions for starting, stoking, and putting out the fire in woodstoves. Chemicals are used to pressure-treat wood; such wood should never be burned indoors. (Because some old gaskets in woodstove doors contain asbestos, when replacing gaskets refer to the instructions in the CPSC, ALA, and EPA booklet, Asbestos in Your Home, to avoid creating an asbestos problem. New gaskets are made of fiberglass.)

Have central air handling systems, including furnaces, flues, and chimneys, inspected annually andpromptly repair cracks or damaged parts.

Blocked, leaking, or damaged chimneys or flues release harmful combustion gases and particles and even fatal concentrations of carbon monoxide. Strictly follow all service and maintenance procedures recommended by the manufacturer, including those that tell you how frequently to change the filter. If manufacturer's instructions are not readily available, change filters once every month or two during periods of use. Proper maintenance is important even for new furnaces because they can also corrode and leak combustion gases, including carbon monoxide.

Read the booklet What You Should Know About Combustion Appliances and Indoor Air Pollution to learn more about combustion pollutants.

HOUSEHOLD PRODUCTS

Organic chemicals are widely used as ingredients in household products. Paints, varnishes, and wax all contain organic solvents, as do many cleaning, disinfecting, cosmetic, degreasing, and hobby products. Fuels are made up of organic chemicals. All of these products can release organic compounds while you are using them, and, to some degree, when they are stored.

EPA's Total Exposure Assessment Methodology (TEAM) studies found levels of about a dozen common organic pollutants to be 2 to 5 times higher inside homes than outside, regardless of whether the homes were located in rural or highly industrial areas. Additional TEAM studies indicate that while people are using products containing organic chemicals, they can expose themselves and others to very high pollutant levels, and elevated concentrations can persist in the air long after the activity is completed.

Health Effects of Household Chemicals

The ability of organic chemicals to cause health effects varies greatly, from those that are highly toxic, to those with no known health effect. As with other pollutants, the extent and nature of the health effect will depend on many factors including level of exposure and length of time exposed. Eye and respiratory tract irritation, headaches, dizziness, visual disorders, and memory impairment are among the immediate symptoms that some people have experienced soon after exposure to some organics. At present, not much is known about what health effects occur from the levels of organics usually found in homes. Many organic compounds are known to cause cancer in animals; some are suspected of causing, or are known to cause, cancer in humans.

Reducing Exposure to Household Chemicals

Follow label instructions carefully.

Potentially hazardous products often have warnings aimed at reducing exposure of the user. For example, if a label says to use the product in a well-ventilated area, go outdoors or in areas equipped with an exhaust fan to use it. Otherwise, open up windows to provide the maximum amount of outdoor air possible.

Throw away partially full containers of old or unneeded chemicals safely.

Because gases can leak even from closed containers, this single step could help lower concentrations of organic chemicals in your home. (Be sure that materials you decide to keep are stored not only in a well-ventilated area but are also safely out of reach of children.) Do not simply toss these unwanted products in the garbage can.

Find out if your local government or any organization in your community sponsors special days for the collection of toxic household wastes. If such days are available, use them to dispose of the unwanted containers safely. If no such collection days are available, think about organizing one.

Buy limited quantities.

If you use products only occasionally or seasonally, such as paints, paint strippers, and kerosene for space heaters or gasoline for lawn mowers, buy only as much as you will use right away.

Keep exposure to emissions from products containing methylene chloride to a minimum.

Consumer products that contain methylene chloride include paint strippers, adhesive removers, and aerosol spray paints. Methylene chloride is known to cause cancer in animals. Also, methylene chloride is converted to carbon monoxide in the body and can cause symptoms associated with exposure to carbon monoxide. Carefully read the labels containing health hazard information and cautions on the proper use of these products. Use products that contain methylene chloride outdoors when possible; use indoors only if the area is well ventilated.

Keep exposure to benzene to a minimum.

Benzene is a known human carcinogen. The main indoor sources of this chemical are environmental tobacco smoke, stored fuels and paint supplies, and automobile emissions in attached garages. Actions that will reduce benzene exposure include eliminating smoking within the home, providing for maximum ventilation during painting, and discarding paint supplies and special fuels that will not be used immediately.

Keep exposure to perchloroethylene emissions from newly dry-cleaned materials to a minimum.

Perchloroethylene is the chemical most widely used in dry cleaning. In laboratory studies, it has been shown to cause cancer in animals. Recent studies indicate that people breathe low levels of this chemical both in homes where dry-cleaned goods are stored and as they wear dry-cleaned clothing. Dry cleaners recapture the perchloroethylene during the dry-cleaning process so they can save money by re-using it, and they remove more of the chemical during the pressing and finishing processes.

Some dry cleaners, however, do not remove as much perchloroethylene as possible all of the time. Taking steps to minimize your exposure to this chemical is prudent. If dry-cleaned goods have a strong chemical odor when you pick them up, do not accept them until they have been properly dried. If goods with a chemical odor are returned to you on subsequent visits, try a different dry cleaner.

FORMALDEHYDE

Formaldehyde is an important chemical used widely by industry to manufacture building materials and numerous household products. It is also a by-product of combustion and certain other natural processes. Thus, it may be present in substantial concentrations both indoors and outdoors.

Sources of formaldehyde in the home include building materials, smoking, household products, and the use of unvented, fuel-burning appliances, like gas stoves or kerosene space heaters. Formaldehyde, by itself or in combination with other chemicals, serves a number of purposes in manufactured products. For example, it is used to add permanent-press qualities to clothing and draperies, as a component of glues and adhesives, and as a preservative in some paints and coating products.

In homes, the most significant sources of formaldehyde are likely to be pressed wood products made using adhesives that contain urea-formaldehyde (UF) resins. Pressed wood products made for indoor use include: particleboard (used as subflooring and shelving and in cabinetry and furniture); hardwood plywood paneling (used for decorative wall covering and used in cabinets and furniture); and medium density fiberboard (used for drawer fronts, cabinets, and furniture tops). Medium density fiberboard contains a higher resin-to-wood ratio than any other UF pressed wood product and is generally recognized as being the highest formaldehyde-emitting pressed wood product.

Other pressed wood products, such as softwood plywood and flake or oriented strandboard, are produced for exterior construction use and contain the dark, or red/black-colored phenol-formaldehyde (PF) resin. Although formaldehyde is present in both types of resins, pressed woods that contain PF resin generally emit formaldehyde at considerably lower rates than those containing UF resin.

Since 1985, the Department of Housing and Urban Development (HUD) has permitted only the use of plywood and particleboard that conform to specified formaldehyde emission limits in the construction of prefabricated and mobile homes. In the past, some of these homes had elevated levels of formaldehyde because of the large amount of high-emitting pressed wood products used in their construction and because of their relatively small interior space.

The rate at which products like pressed wood or textiles release formaldehyde can change. Formaldehyde emissions will generally decrease as products age. When the products are new, high indoor temperatures or humidity can cause increased release of formaldehyde from these products.

During the 1970s, many homeowners had urea-formaldehyde foam insulation (UFFI) installed in the wall cavities of their homes as an energy conservation measure. However, many of these homes were found to have relatively high indoor concentrations of formaldehyde soon after the UFFI installation. Few homes are now being insulated with this product. Studies show that formaldehyde emissions from UFFI decline with time; therefore, homes in which UFFI was installed many years ago are unlikely to have high levels of formaldehyde now.

Health Effects of Formaldehyde

Formaldehyde, a colorless, pungent-smelling gas, can cause watery eyes, burning sensations in the eyes and throat, nausea, and difficulty in breathing in some humans exposed at elevated levels (above 0.1 parts per million). High concentrations may trigger attacks in people with asthma. There is evidence that some people can develop a sensitivity to formaldehyde. It has also been shown to cause cancer in animals and may cause cancer in humans.

Reducing Exposure to Formaldehyde in Homes

Ask about the formaldehyde content of pressed wood products,including building materials, cabinetry, and furniture before you purchase them.

If you experience adverse reactions to formaldehyde, you may want to avoid the use of pressed wood products and other formaldehyde-emitting goods. Even if you do not experience such reactions, you may wish to reduce your exposure as much as possible by purchasing exterior-grade products, which emit less formaldehyde.

Some studies suggest that coating pressed wood products with polyurethane may reduce formaldehyde emissions for some period of time. To be effective, any such coating must cover all surfaces and edges and remain intact. Increase the ventilation and carefully follow the manufacturernstructions while applying these coatings. (If you are sensitive to formaldehyde, check the label contents before purchasing coating products to avoid buying products that contain formaldehyde, as they will emit the chemical for a short time after application.) Maintain moderate temperature and humidity levels and provide adequate ventilation. The rate at which formaldehyde is released is accelerated by heat and may also depend somewhat on the humidity level. Therefore, the use of dehumidifiers and air conditioning to control humidity and to maintain a moderate temperature can help reduce formaldehyde emissions. (Drain and clean dehumidifier collection trays frequently so that they do not become a breeding ground for microorganisms.) Increasing the rate of ventilation in your home will also help in reducing formaldehyde levels.

PESTICIDES

According to a recent survey, 75 percent of U.S. households used at least one pesticide product indoors during the past year. Products used most often are insecticides and disinfectants. Another study suggests that 80 percent of most people's exposure to pesticides occurs indoors and that measurable levels of up to a dozen pesticides have been found in the air inside homes. The amount of pesticides found in homes appears to be greater than can be explained by recent pesticide use in those households; other possible sources include contaminated soil or dust that floats or is tracked in from outside, stored pesticide containers, and household surfaces that collect and then release the pesticides. Pesticides used in and around the home include products to control insects (insecticides), termites (termiticides), rodents (rodenticides), fungi (fungicides), and microbes (disinfectants). They are sold as sprays, liquids, sticks, powders, crystals, balls, and foggers.

In 1990, the American Association of Poison Control Centers reported that some 79,000 children were involved in common household pesticide poisonings or exposures. In households with children under five years old, almost one-half stored at least one pesticide product within reach of children.

EPA registers pesticides for use and requires manufacturers to put information on the label about when and how to use the pesticide. It is important to remember that the "-cide" in pesticides means "to kill." These products can be dangerous if not used properly.

In addition to the active ingredient, pesticides are also made up of ingredients that are used to carry the active agent. These carrier agents are called "inerts" in pesticides because they are not toxic to the targeted pest; nevertheless, some inerts are capable of causing health problems.

Health Effects from Pesticides

Both the active and inert ingredients in pesticides can be organic compounds; therefore, both could add to the levels of airborne organics inside homes. Both types of ingredients can cause the effects discussed in this document under "Household Products," however, as with other household products, there is insufficient understanding at present about what pesticide concentrations are necessary to produce these effects.

Exposure to high levels of cyclodiene pesticides, commonly associated with misapplication, has produced various symptoms, including headaches, dizziness, muscle twitching, weakness, tingling sensations, and nausea. In addition, EPA is concerned that cyclodienes might cause long-term damage to the liver and the central nervous system, as well as an increased risk of cancer.

There is no further sale or commercial use permitted for the following cyclodiene or related pesticides: chlordane, aldrin, dieldrin, and heptachlor. The only exception is the use of heptachlor by utility companies to control fire ants in underground cable boxes.

Reducing Exposure to Pesticides in Homes

Read the label and follow the directions. It is illegal to use any pesticide in any manner inconsistent with the directions on its label.

Unless you have had special training and are certified, never use a pesticide that is restricted to use by state-certified pest control operators. Such pesticides are simply too dangerous for application by a noncertified person. Use only the pesticides approved for use by the general public and then only in recommended amounts; increasing the amount does not offer more protection against pests and can be harmful to you and your plants and pets.

Ventilate the Area well After Pesticide Use

Mix or dilute pesticides outdoors or in a well-ventilated area and only in the amounts that will be immediately needed. If possible, take plants and pets outside when applying pesticides to them.

Use nonchemical methods of pest control when possible.

Since pesticides can be found far from the site of their original application, it is prudent to reduce the use of chemical pesticides outdoors as well as indoors. Depending on the site and pest to be controlled, one or more of the following steps can be effective: use of biological pesticides, such as Bacillus thuringiensis, for the control of gypsy moths; selection of disease-resistant plants; and frequent washing of indoor plants and pets. Termite damage can be reduced or prevented by making certain that wooden building materials do not come into direct contact with the soil and by storing firewood away from the home. By appropriately fertilizing, watering, and aerating lawns, the need for chemical pesticide treatments of lawns can be dramatically reduced.

If you decide to use a pest control company, choose one carefully.

Ask for an inspection of your home and get a written control program for evaluation before you sign a contract. The control program should list specific names of pests to be controlled and chemicals to be used; it should also reflect any of your safety concerns. Insist on a proven record of competence and customer satisfaction.

Dispose of unwanted pesticides safely.

If you have unused or partially used pesticide containers you want to get rid of, dispose of them according to the directions on the label or on special household hazardous waste collection days. If there are no such collection days in your community, work with others to organize them.

Keep exposure to moth repellents to a minimum.

One pesticide often found in the home is paradichlorobenzene, a commonly used active ingredient in moth repellents. This chemical is known to cause cancer in animals, but substantial scientific uncertainty exists over the effects, if any, of long-term human exposure to paradichlorobenzene. EPA requires that products containing paradichlorobenzene bear warnings such as "avoid breathing vapors" to warn users of potential short-term toxic effects. Where possible, paradichlorobenzene, and items to be protected against moths, should be placed in trunks or other containers that can be stored in areas that are separately ventilated from the home, such as attics and detached garages. Paradichlorobenzene is also the key active ingredient in many air fresheners (in fact, some labels for moth repellents recommend that these same products be used as air fresheners or deodorants). Proper ventilation and basic household cleanliness will go a long way toward preventing unpleasant odors.

ASBESTOS

Asbestos is a mineral fiber that has been used commonly in a variety of building construction materials for insulation and as a fire-retardant. EPA and CPSC have banned several asbestos products. Manufacturers have also voluntarily limited uses of asbestos. Today, asbestos is most commonly found in older homes, in pipe and furnace insulation materials, asbestos shingles, millboard, textured paints and other coating materials, and floor tiles.

Elevated concentrations of airborne asbestos can occur after asbestos-containing materials are disturbed by cutting, sanding or other remodeling activities. Improper attempts to remove these materials can release asbestos fibers into the air in homes, increasing asbestos levels and endangering people living in those homes.

Health Effects of Asbestos

The most dangerous asbestos fibers are too small to be visible. After they are inhaled, they can remain and accumulate in the lungs. Asbestos can cause lung cancer, meso-thelioma (a cancer of the chest and abdominal linings), and asbestosis (irreversible lung scarring that can be fatal). Symptoms of these diseases do not show up until many years after exposure began. Most people with asbestos-related diseases were exposed to elevated concentrations on the job; some developed disease from exposure to clothing and equipment brought home from job sites.

Reducing Exposure to Asbestos in Homes

Learn how asbestos problems are created in homes.

If you think your home may have asbestos, dont panic!

Usually it is best to leave asbestos material that is in good condition alone. Generally, material in good condition will not release asbestos fiber. There is no danger unless fibers are released and inhaled into the lungs.

Do not cut, rip, or sand asbestos-containing materials.

Leave undamaged materials alone and, to the extent possible, prevent them from being damaged, disturbed, or touched. Periodically inspect for damage or deterioration.

Discard damaged or worn asbestos gloves, stove-top pads, or ironing board covers. Check with local health, environmental, or other appropriate officials to find out about proper handling and disposal procedures.

If asbestos material is more than slightly damaged, or if you are going to make changes in your home that might disturb it, repair or removal by a professional is needed. Before you have your house remodeled, find out whether asbestos materials are present. When you need to remove or clean up asbestos, use a professionally trained contractor.

Select a contractor only after careful discussion of the problems in your home and the steps the contractor will take to clean up or remove them. Consider the option of sealing off the materials instead of removing them.

Call EPA's TSCA assistance line (202-554-1404) to find out whether your state has a training and certification program for asbestos removal contractors and for information on EPA's asbestos programs.

LEAD

Lead has long been recognized as a harmful environmental pollutant. In late 1991, the Secretary of the Department of Health and Human Services called lead the "number one environmental threat to the health of children in the United States." There are many ways in which humans are exposed to lead: through air, drinking water, food, contaminated soil, deteriorating paint, and dust. Airborne lead enters the body when an individual breathes or swallows lead particles or dust once it has settled. Before it was known how harmful lead could be, it was used in paint, gasoline, water pipes, and many other products.

Old lead-based paint is the most significant source of lead exposure in the U.S. today. Harmful exposures to lead can be created when lead-based paint is improperly removed from surfaces by dry scraping, sanding, or open-flame burning. High concentrations of airborne lead particles in homes can also result from lead dust from outdoor sources, including contaminated soil tracked inside, and use of lead in certain indoor activities such as soldering and stained-glass making.

Health Effects of Exposure to Lead

Lead affects practically all systems within the body. At high levels it can cause convulsions, coma, and even death. Lower levels of lead can adversely affect the brain, central nervous system, blood cells, and kidneys.

The effects of lead exposure on fetuses and young children can be severe. They include delays in physical and mental development, lower IQ levels, shortened attention spans, and increased behavioral problems. Fetuses, infants, and children are more vulnerable to lead exposure than adults since lead is more easily absorbed into growing bodies, and the tissues of small children are more sensitive to the damaging effects of lead. Children may have higher exposures since they are more likely to get lead dust on their hands and then put their fingers or other lead-contaminated objects into their mouths.

Get your child tested for lead exposure. To find out where to do this, call your doctor or local health clinic. For more information on health effects, get a copy of the Centers for Disease Control's, Preventing Lead Poisoning in Young Children (October 1991).

Ways to Reduce Exposure to Lead

Keep areas where children play as dust-free and clean as possible.

Mop floors and wipe window ledges and chewable surfaces such as cribs with a solution of powdered automatic dishwasher detergent in warm water. (Dishwasher detergents are recommended because of their high content of phosphate.) Most multi-purpose cleaners will not remove lead in ordinary dust. Wash toys and stuffed animals regularly. Make sure that children wash their hands before meals, nap time, and bedtime.

Reduce the risk from lead-based paint.

Most homes built before 1960 contain heavily leaded paint. Some homes built as recently as 1978 may also contain lead paint. This paint could be on window frames, walls, the outside of homes, or other surfaces. Do not burn painted wood since it may contain lead.

Leave lead-based paint undisturbed if it is in good condition-do not sand or burn off paint that may contain lead.

Lead paint in good condition is usually not a problem except in places where painted surfaces rub against each other and create dust (for example, opening a window).

Do not remove lead paint yourself.

Individuals have been poisoned by scraping or sanding lead paint because these activities generate large amounts of lead dust. Consult your state health or housing department for suggestions on which private laboratories or public agencies may be able to help test your home for lead in paint. Home test kits cannot detect small amounts of lead under some conditions. Hire a person with special training for correcting lead paint problems to remove lead-based paint. Occupants, especially children and pregnant women, should leave the building until all work is finished and clean-up is done.

For additional information dealing with lead-based paint abatement contact the Department of Housing and Urban Development for the following two documents: Comprehensive and Workable Plan for the Abatement of

Lead-Based Paint in Privately Owned Housing: Report to Congress (December 7, 1990) and Lead-Based Paint: Interim Guidelines for Hazard Identification and Abatement in Public and Indian Housing (September 1990).

Do not bring lead dust into the home.

If you work in construction, demolition, painting, with batteries, in a radiator repair shop or lead factory, or your hobby involves lead, you may unknowingly bring lead into your home on your hands or clothes. You may also be tracking in lead from soil around your home. Soil very close to homes may be contaminated from lead paint on the outside of the building. Soil by roads and highways may be contaminated from years of exhaust fumes from cars and trucks that used leaded gas. Use door mats to wipe your feet before entering the home. If you work with lead in your job or a hobby, change your clothes before you go home and wash these clothes separately. Encourage your children to play in sand and grassy areas instead of dirt which sticks to fingers and toys. Try to keep your children from eating dirt, and make sure they wash their hands when they come inside.

Find out about lead in drinking water.

Most well and city water does not usually contain lead. Water usually picks up lead inside the home from household plumbing that is made with lead materials. The only way to know if there is lead in drinking water is to have it tested. Contact the local health department or the water supplier to find out how to get the water tested. Send for the EPA pamphlet, Lead and Your Drinking Water, for more information about what you can do if you have lead in your drinking water.

Eat right.

A child who gets enough iron and calcium will absorb less lead. Foods rich in iron include eggs, red meats, and beans.

Dairy products are high in calcium. Do not store food or liquid in lead crystal glassware or imported or old pottery. If you reuse old plastic bags to store or carry food, keep the printing on the outside of the bag.

WHAT ABOUT CARPET?

In recent years, a number of consumers have associated a variety of symptoms with the installation of new carpet. Scientists have not been able to determine whether the chemicals emitted by new carpets are responsible. If you are installing new carpet, you may wish to take the following steps:

- Talk to your carpet retailer. Ask for information on emissions from carpet.
- Ask the retailer to unroll and air out the carpet in a well-ventilated area before installation.
- Ask for low-emitting adhesives if adhesives are needed.
- Consider leaving the premises during and immediately after carpet installation. You may wish to schedule the installation when most family members or office workers are out.
- Be sure the retailer requires the installer to follow the Carpet and Rug Institute's installation guidelines.
- Open doors and windows. Increasing the amount of fresh air in the home will reduce exposure to most chemicals released from carpet. During and after installation, use window fans, room air conditioners, or other mechanical ventilation equipment you may have installed in your house, to exhaust fumes to the outdoors. Keep them running for 48 to 72 hours after the new carpet is installed.
- Contact your carpet retailer if objectionable odors persist.

- Follow the manufacturer's instructions for proper carpet maintenance.

WHEN BUILDING A NEW HOME

Building a new home provides the opportunity for preventing indoor air problems. However, it can result in exposure to higher levels of indoor air contaminants if careful attention is not given to potential pollution sources and the air exchange rate.

Express your concerns about indoor air quality to your architect or builder and enlist his or her cooperation in taking measures to provide good indoor air quality. Talk both about purchasing building materials and furnishings that are low-emitting and about providing an adequate amount of ventilation.

The American Society of Heating, Refrigerating, and Air-Conditioning Engineers (ASHRAE) recommends a ventilation rate of 0.35 ach (air changes per hour) for new homes, and some new homes are built to even tighter specifications. Particular care should be given in such homes to preventing the build-up of indoor air pollutants to high levels.

Here are a few important actions that can make a difference:

Use radon-resistant construction techniques.

Choose building materials and furnishings that will keep indoor air pollution to a minimum.

There are many actions a homeowner can take to select products that will prevent indoor air problems from occurring-a couple of them are mentioned here. First, use exterior-grade pressed wood products made with phenol-formaldehyde resin in floors, cabinetry, and wall surfaces. Or, as an alternative, consider using solid wood products. Secondly, if you plan to install wall-to-wall carpet on concrete in contact with the ground, especially concrete in basements, make sure that an effective moisture barrier is installed prior to installing the carpet. Do not permanently adhere carpet to concrete with adhesives so that the carpet can be removed if it becomes wet.

Provide proper drainage and seal foundations in new construction.

Air that enters the home through the foundation can contain more moisture than is generated from all occupant activities.

Become familiar with mechanical ventilation systems and consider installing one.

Advanced designs of new homes are starting to feature mechanical systems that bring outdoor air into the home. Some of these designs include energy-efficient heat recovery ventilators (also known as air-to-air heat exchangers).

Ensure that combustion appliances, including furnaces, fireplaces, woodstoves, and heaters, are properly vented and receive enough supply air.

Combustion gases, including carbon monoxide, and particles can be back-drafted from the chimney or flue into the living space if the combustion appliance is not properly vented or does not receive enough supply air. Back-drafting can be a particular problem in weatherized or tightly constructed homes. Installing a dedicated outdoor air supply for the combustion appliance can help prevent backdrafting.

DO YOU SUSPECT YOUR OFFICE HAS AN INDOOR AIR PROBLEM?

Indoor air quality problems are not limited to homes. In fact, many office buildings have significant air pollution sources. Some of these buildings may be inadequately ventilated. For example, mechanical ventilation systems may not be designed or operated to provide adequate amounts of outdoor air. Finally, people generally have less control over the indoor environment in their offices than they do in their homes. As a result, there has been an increase in the incidence of reported health problems.

Health Effects

A number of well-identified illnesses, such as Legionnaires' disease, asthma, hypersensitivity pneumonitis, and humidifier fever, have been directly traced to specific building problems. These are called building-related illnesses. Most of these diseases can be treated, nevertheless, some pose serious risks.

Sometimes, however, building occupants experience symptoms that do not fit the pattern of any particular illness and are difficult to trace to any specific source. This phenomenon has been labeled sick building syndrome. People may complain of one or more of the following symptoms: dry or burning mucous membranes in the nose, eyes, and throat; sneezing; stuffy or runny nose; fatigue or lethargy; headache; dizziness; nausea; irritability and forgetfulness. Poor lighting, noise, vibration, thermal discomfort, and psychological stress may also cause, or contribute to, these symptoms.

There is no single manner in which these health problems appear. In some cases, problems begin as workers enter their offices and diminish as workers leave; other times, symptoms continue until the illness is treated. Sometimes there are outbreaks of illness among many workers in a single building; in other cases, health symptoms show up only in individual workers.

In the opinion of some World Health Organization experts, up to 30 percent of new or remodeled commercial buildings may have unusually high rates of health and comfort complaints from occupants that may potentially be related to indoor air quality.

What Causes Problems?

Three major reasons for poor indoor air quality in office buildings are the presence of indoor air pollution sources; poorly designed, maintained, or operated ventilation systems; and uses of the building that were unanticipated or poorly planned for when the building was designed or renovated.

Sources of Office Air Pollution

As with homes, the most important factor influencing indoor air quality is the presence of pollutant sources. Commonly found office pollutants and their sources include environmental tobacco smoke; asbestos from insulating and fire-retardant building supplies; formaldehyde from pressed wood products; other organics from building materials, carpet, and other office furnishings, cleaning materials and activities, restroom air fresheners, paints, adhesives, copying machines, and photography and print shops; biological contaminants from dirty ventilation systems or water-damaged walls, ceilings, and carpets; and pesticides from pest management practices.

Ventilation Systems

Mechanical ventilation systems in large buildings are designed and operated not only to heat and cool the air, but also to draw in and circulate outdoor air. If they are poorly designed, operated, or maintained, however, ventilation systems can contribute to indoor air problems in several ways.

For example, problems arise when, in an effort to save energy, ventilation systems are not used to bring in adequate amounts of outdoor air. Inadequate ventilation also occurs if the air supply and return vents within each room are blocked or placed in such a way that outdoor air does not actually reach the breathing zone of building occupants. Improperly located outdoor air intake vents can also bring in air contaminated with automobile and truck exhaust, boiler emissions, fumes from dumpsters, or air vented from restrooms. Finally, ventilation systems can be a source of in door pollution themselves by spreading biological contaminants that have multiplied in cooling towers, humidifiers, dehumidifiers, air conditioners, or the inside surfaces of ventilation duct work.

Use of the Building

Indoor air pollutants can be circulated from portions of the building used for specialized purposes, such as restaurants, print shops, and dry-cleaning stores, into offices in the same building. Carbon monoxide and other components of automobile exhaust can be drawn from underground parking garages through stairwells and elevator shafts into office spaces.

In addition, buildings originally designed for one purpose may end up being converted to use as office space. If not properly modified during building renovations, the room partitions and ventilation system can contribute to indoor air quality problems by restricting air recirculation or by providing an inadequate supply of outdoor air.

What to do if You Suspect a Problem

If you or others at your office are experiencing health or comfort problems that you suspect may be caused by indoor air pollution, you can do the following:

- Talk with other workers, your supervisor, and union representatives to see if the problems are being experienced by others and urge that a record of reported health complaints be kept by management, if one has not already been established.

- Talk with your own physician and report your problems to the company physician, nurse, or health and safety officer.
- Call your state or local health department or air pollution control agency to talk over the symptoms and possible causes.
- Encourage building management to obtain a copy of Building Air Quality: A Guide for Building Owners and Facility Managers from the EPA. Building Air Quality (BAQ) is simply written, yet provides comprehensive information for identifying, correcting, and preventing indoor air quality problems. BAQ also provides supporting information such as when and how to select outside technical assistance, how to communicate with others regarding indoor air issues, and where to find additional sources of information.
- Frequently, indoor air quality problems in large commercial buildings cannot be effectively identified or remedied without a comprehensive building investigation. These investigations may start with written questionnaires and telephone consultations in which building investigators assess the history of occupant symptoms and building operation procedures. In some cases, these inquiries may quickly uncover the problem and on-site visits are unnecessary.
- More often, however, investigators will need to come to the building to conduct personal interviews with occupants, to look for possible sources of the problems, and to inspect the design and operation of the ventilation system and other building features. Because taking measurements of pollutants at the very low levels often found in office buildings is

expensive and may not yield information readily useful in identifying problem sources, investigators may not take many measurements. The process of solving indoor air quality problems that result in health and comfort complaints can be a slow one, involving several trial solutions before successful remedial actions are identified.

- If a professional company is hired to conduct a building investigation, select a company on the basis of its experience in identifying and solving indoor air quality problems in nonindustrial buildings.
- Work with others to establish a smoking policy that eliminates involuntary nonsmoker exposure to environmental tobacco smoke.

MAJOR INDOOR AIR POLLUTANTS IN THE HOME

The pollutants listed in this guide have been shown to cause the health effects mentioned. However, it is not necessarily true that the effects noted occur at the pollutant concentration levels typically found in the home. In many cases, our understanding of the pollutants and their health effects is too limited to determine the levels at which the listed effects could occur.

RADON (RN)

Sources: Earth and rock beneath home; well water; building materials.

Health Effects: No immediate symptoms. Estimated to contribute to between 7,000 and 30,000 lung cancer deaths each year. Smokers are at higher risk of developing radon-induced lung cancer.

Levels in Homes: Based on a national residential radon survey completed in 1991, the average indoor radon level is

1.3 picocuries per liter (pCi/L). The average outdoor level is about 0.4 pCi/L.

Steps to Reduce Exposure:

- Test your home for radcn_it's easy and inexpensive.
- Fix your home if your radon level is 4 picocuries per liter (pCi/L) or higher.
- Radon levels less than 4 pCi/L still pose a risk, and in many cases may be reduced.
- If you want more information on radon, contact your state radon office, or call 800-SOS-RADON.

ENVIRONMENTAL TOBACCO SMOKE (ETS)

Source: Cigarette, pipe, and cigar smoking.

Health Effects: Eye, nose, and throat irritation; headaches; lung cancer; may contribute to heart disease. Specifically for children, increased risk of lower respiratory tract infections, such as bronchitis and pneumonia, and ear infections; build-up of fluid in the middle ear; increased severity and frequency of asthma episodes; decreased lung function.

Levels in Homes: Particle levels in homes without smokers or other strong particle sources are the same as, or lower than, those outdoors. Homes with one or more smokers may have particle levels several times higher than outdoor levels.

Steps to Reduce Exposure:

- Do not smoke in your home or permit others to do so.
- Do not smoke if children are present, particularly infants and toddlers.
- If smoking indoors cannot be avoided, increase ventilation in the area where smoking takes place. Open windows or use exhaust fans.

BIOLOGICALS

Sources: Wet or moist walls, ceilings, carpets, and furniture; poorly maintained humidifiers, dehumidifiers, and air conditioners; bedding; household pets.

Health Effects: Eye, nose, and throat irritation; shortness of breath; dizziness; lethargy; fever; digestive problems. Can cause asthma; humidifier fever; influenza and other infectious diseases.

Levels in Homes: Indoor levels of pollen and fungi are lower than outdoor levels (except where indoor sources of fungi are present). Indoor levels of dust mites are higher than outdoor levels.

Steps to Reduce Exposure:

- Install and use fans vented to outdoors in kitchens and bathrooms.
- Vent clothes dryers to outdoors.
- Clean cool mist and ultrasonic humidifiers in accordance with manufacturer's instructions and refill with clean water daily.
- Empty water trays in air conditioners, dehumidifiers, and refrigerators frequently.
- Clean and dry or remove water-damaged carpets.
- Use basements as living areas only if they are leakproof and have adequate ventilation. Use dehumidifiers, if necessary, to maintain humidity between 30-50 percent.

CARBON MONOXIDE (CO)

Sources: Unvented kerosene and gas space heaters; leaking chimneys and furnaces; back-drafting from furnaces, gas water heaters, woodstoves, and fireplaces; gas stoves.

Automobile exhaust from attached garages. Environmental Tobacco Smoke.

Health Effects: At low concentrations, fatigue in healthy people and chest pain in people with heart disease. At higher concentrations, impaired vision and coordination; headaches; dizziness; confusion; nausea. Can cause flu-like symptoms that clear up after leaving home. Fatal at very high concentrations.

Levels in Homes: Average levels in homes without gas stoves vary from 0.5 to 5 parts per million (ppm). Levels near properly adjusted gas stoves are often 5 to 15 ppm and those near poorly adjusted stoves may be 30 ppm or higher.

Steps to Reduce Exposure:

- Keep gas appliances properly adjusted.
- Consider purchasing a vented space heater when replacing an unvented one.
- Use proper fuel in kerosene space heaters.
- Install and use an exhaust fan vented to outdoors over gas stoves.
- Open flues when fireplaces are in use.
- Choose properly sized woodstoves that are certified to meet EPA emission standards. Make certain that doors on all woodstoves fit tightly.
- Have a trained professional inspect, clean, and tune-up central heating system (furnaces, flues, and chimneys) annually. Repair any leaks promptly.
- Do not idle the car inside garage.

NITROGEN DIOXIDE (NO_2)

Sources: Kerosene heaters, unvented gas stoves and heaters. Environmental tobacco smoke. Health Effects: Eye, nose, and throat irritation. May cause impaired lung function and increased respiratory infections in young children.

Levels in Homes: Average level in homes without combustion appliances is about half that of outdoors. In homes with gas stoves, kerosene heaters, or unvented gas space heaters, indoor levels often exceed outdoor levels.

Steps to Reduce Exposure: See steps under carbon monoxide.

ORGANIC GASES

Sources: Household products including: paints, paint strippers, and other solvents; wood preservatives; aerosol sprays; cleansers and disinfectants; moth repellents and air fresheners; stored fuels and automotive products; hobby supplies; dry-cleaned clothing.

Health Effects: Eye, nose, and throat irritation; headaches, loss of coordination, nausea; damage to liver, kidney, and central nervous system. Some organics can cause cancer in animals; some are suspected or known to cause cancer in humans.

Levels in Homes: Studies have found that levels of several organics average 2 to 5 times higher indoors than outdoors. During and for several hours immediately after certain activities, such as paint stripping, levels may be 1,000 times background outdoor levels.

Steps to Reduce Exposure:

- Use household products according to manufac-turer's directions.
- Make sure you provide plenty of fresh air when using these products.
- Throw away unused or little-used containers safely; buy in quantities that you will use soon.

- Keep out of reach of children and pets.
- Never mix household care products unless directed on the label.

RESPIRABLE PARTICLES

Sources: Fireplaces, woodstoves, and kerosene heaters. Environmental tobacco smoke.

Health Effects: Eye, nose, and throat irritation; respiratory infections and bronchitis; lung cancer. (Effects attributable to environmental tobacco smoke are listed elsewhere.)

Levels in Homes: Particle levels in homes without smoking or other strong particle sources are the same as, or lower than, outdoor levels.

Steps to Reduce Exposure:

- Vent all furnaces to outdoors; keep doors to rest of house open when using unvented space heaters.
- Choose properly sized woodstoves, certified to meet EPA emission standards; make certain that doors on all woodstoves fit tightly.
- Have a trained professional inspect, clean, and tune-up central heating system (furnace, flues, and chimneys) annually. Repair any leaks promptly.
- Change filters on central heating and cooling systems and air cleaners according to manufacturer's directions.

FORMALDEHYDE

Sources: Pressed wood products (hardwood plywood wall paneling, particleboard, fiberboard) and furniture made with these pressed wood products. Urea-formaldehyde foam insulation (UFFI). Combustion sources and environmental tobacco smoke. Durable press drapes, other textiles, and glues.

Health Effects: Eye, nose, and throat irritation; wheezing and coughing; fatigue; skin rash; severe allergic reactions. May cause cancer. May also cause other effects listed under "organic gases."

Levels in Homes: Average concentrations in older homes without UFFI are generally well below 0.1 (ppm). In homes with significant amounts of new pressed wood products, levels can be greater than 0.3 ppm.

Steps to Reduce Exposure:

- Use "exterior-grade" pressed wood products (lower-emitting because they contain phenol resins, not urea resins).
- Use air conditioning and dehumidifiers to maintain moderate temperature and reduce humidity levels.
- Increase ventilation, particularly after bringing new sources of formaldehyde into the home.

PESTICIDES

Sources: Products used to kill household pests (insecticides, termiticides, and disinfectants). Also, products used on lawns and gardens that drift or are tracked inside the house.

Health Effects: Irritation to eye, nose, and throat; damage to central nervous system and kidney; increased risk of cancer.

Levels in Homes: Preliminary research shows widespread presence of pesticide residues in homes.

Steps to Reduce Exposure:

- Use strictly according to manufacturer's directions.

- Mix or dilute outdoors.
- Apply only in recommended quantities.
- Increase ventilation when using indoors. Take plants or pets outdoors when applying pesticides to them.
- Use nonchemical methods of pest control where possible.
- If you use a pest control company, select it carefully.
- Do not store unneeded pesticides inside home; dispose of unwanted containers safely.
- Store clothes with moth repellents in separately ventilated areas, if possible.
- Keep indoor spaces clean, dry, and well ventilated to avoid pest and odor problems.

ASBESTOS

Sources: Deteriorating, damaged, or disturbed insulation, fireproofing, acoustical materials, and floor tiles.

Health Effects: No immediate symptoms, but long-term risk of chest and abdominal cancers and lung diseases. Smokers are at higher risk of developing asbestos-induced lung cancer.

Levels in Homes: Elevated levels can occur in homes where asbestos-containing materials are damaged or disturbed.

Steps to Reduce Exposure:

- It is best to leave undamaged asbestos material alone if it is not likely to be disturbed.
- Use trained and qualified contractors for control measures that may disturb asbestos and for cleanup.
- Follow proper procedures in replacing woodstove door gaskets that may contain asbestos.

LEAD

Sources: Lead-based paint, contaminated soil, dust, and drinking water.

Health Effects: Lead affects practically all systems within the body. Lead at high levels (lead levels at or above 80 micrograms per deciliter (80 ug/dl) of blood) can cause convulsions, coma, and even death. Lower levels of lead can cause adverse health effects on the central nervous system, kidney, and blood cells. Blood lead levels as low as 10 ug/dl can impair mental and physical development.

Steps to Reduce Exposure:

- Keep areas where children play as dust-free and clean as possible.
- Leave lead-based paint undisturbed if it is in good condition; do not sand or burn off paint that may contain lead.
- Do not remove lead paint yourself.
- Do not bring lead dust into the home.
- If your work or hobby involves lead, change clothes and use doormats before entering your home.
- Eat a balanced diet, rich in calcium and iron.

6

AN ASSESSMENT OF THE HEAVY METAL POLLUTION

INTRODUCTION

Tidal marshes (salt-marshes) are of environ-mental and economic importance, offering impor-tant wildlife habitats and feeding grounds (Doody 1992) and providing nutrient sources for estuarine and offshore fisheries. The pollution of tidal marshes may create far-reaching repercussions in near-shore biological and chemical systems. Deteri-oration in the vegetative cover owing to pollution may ultimately facilitate the decline of the tidal marsh by erosion. Consequently, a reduction in the ability of the marsh to buffer the energy of the sea may pose a threat to coastal defence.

The west coast of Ireland is often perceived as a 'clean' environment which has avoided the de-gree of environmental degradation experienced by many developed countries and even by the tidal marshes and estuaries of the east coast of Ireland. Few investigations of coastal pollution on the west coast of Ireland have been carried out, and the authors know of none pertaining to heavy metals. The value of commercial fisheries, the general amenity value and the tourist potential of Ireland's coastal regions are regarded as 'considerable', and consequently the pressure to maintain coastal resources in their current state is high.

Most littoral marine pollution studies have been performed on subtidal near-shore environments. Fewer studies have examined the heavy metal pollutants in tidal flats or tidal marshes. This chapter will assess the level of heavy metal pollution at two tidal flats and adjacent marshes on the north-west coast of Ireland and investigate the processes affecting their concentra-tions across the tidal gradient of the upper shore-line. There are five main sources of heavy metals in aquatic and sedimentary systems: erosion of geo-logical sources, industrial processing of ores and metals, the use of metals and metal compounds in industry, the burning of fossil fuels, and leaching from refuse dumps. Heavy metals are classed as a conservative pollutant in that they are not dissipated by microbial attack and remain available in variable degrees to plants and animals, sometimes with harmful effects.

The widespread use of heavy metals in indus-tries ranging from large-scale mining to intensive agriculture has resulted in a variety of heavy metals being released into the environment to concentra-tions in excess of the natural background levels. The potential environmental damage might be comparatively small if these metals are ultimately fixed in sediments and pore-water concentrations limited by their solubility. However, the decay of organic matter may enhance the harmful potential of the heavy metals as the ensuing reducing conditions can mobilise heavy metals, which become concentrated by physical or chemical processes.

Heavy metals entering the aquatic and sedi-mentary environments can do so in a variety of chemical forms. Suspended matter tends to preferentially adsorb heavy metals in water and to provide the main mode of heavy metal emplacement in estuarine settings. In unpol-luted areas those heavy metals detected by a total metal ion method may have their origin in the parent material of the sediment. In heavily polluted areas these fractions will be present in addition to any pollutant that may exist. The heavy metals that are present in other chemical forms will be dis-tributed between the organic matter and hydrous manganese and iron oxides. Therefore, in order to assess any anthropogenic pollution, the indicator metals chosen must be present as background spe-cies and as potential pollutants.

This investigation analysed intertidal, tidal marsh edge and supratidal sediment samples from two marshes for the five heavy metals: lead, cop-per, zinc, chromium and manganese. The degree of variation in particle size, sediment type (includ-ing measures of organic carbon, sand, silt and clay) and tidal immersion histories was also analysed, allowing us to gain insight into the processes affecting the representation of pollution histories and the concentration of heavy metals.

MATERIALS AND METHODS

Site Descriptions

The two sites were chosen at locations on the north-west coast of Ireland where we suspected anthropogenic heavy metal inputs to be representative of levels of these heavy metals for this part of the coast. The catchments for both tidal marsh sites are indicated.

Bracky Bridge

Bracky Bridge, Co. Donegal, is located about 55km north of Donegal town, near to the village of Ardara. The tidal marsh is at the head of a narrow estuary (Loughros Beg), 7.5km from the open sea. Loughros Beg narrows from 1.6km at the mouth to almost 250m at the head. The nearest predicted mean spring and neap tidal ranges are 3.5m and 1.5m respectively, with mean high-water springs at 1.7m OD; OD refers to Ordnance Datum at Malin Head. At low tide, the intertidal areas are exposed to reveal extensive sand and mudflats. The Bracky River flows into the head of the estuary and forms the easterly and northerly limit to the site, draining a mountainous catchment. The mean annual rainfall in this catchment is approximately 1600mm/yr. The tidal marsh is subject to infrequent grazing by cattle and possesses a cliffed edge showing limited read-justment since 1835 according to map evidence. The marsh increases in eleva-tion landward from 1.5m to 2.56m OD, allowing increased tidal inundation at the tidal marsh edge. Juncus maritima covers large areas of the marsh, with tidal marsh grasses (e.g. Puccinellia maritima) dominant at more seaward localities. Backmarsh areas, only inundated by high spring tides and storm surges, are dominated by bryophytes.

SAMPLE COLLECTION AND ANALYSIS

Cores were collected from both sites using square PVC tubing (6cm×6cm×100cm) during February 1995 from the tidal flats (BBA and STA), the seaward cliffed edge of the tidal marsh (BBB and STB), and the supratidal (BBC) and backmarsh (STC) areas (Fig. 2a and b). The suffixes BB and ST refer to Bracky Bridge and Streamstown re-spectively. The depth of the core from the tidal flat at Streamstown (STA) was limited to 42cm owing to the presence of an impenetrable gravel layer.

Cores were opened in the laboratory, profiles described and continuously sampled at 2cm intervals. The edges of the samples were trimmed and subsamples stored in a refrigerator awaiting analy-sis. Before each analysis the samples were oven-dried at 50°C until no further weight loss was observed. The dried samples were stored in a dessicator until required.

Prior to grain size analysis, carbonates (includ-ing shell fragments and other acid soluble detrital fragments) were removed by dissolution in 10% hydrochloric acid. Organic carbon was removed from the samples by loss-on-ignition at 585°C for 2-3 hours, with peaty samples combusted for longer

(Dean 1974). Samples were allowed to cool in a dessicator and the weight loss recorded. Grain size analysis was carried out using the Galai Cis-1 laser particle-size analyser (Jantschik et al. 1992) after particles greater than 1mm in diame-ter were removed by sieving. The weight of this fraction was recorded and included in the final percentage sand, silt and clay textural calculations.

The percentage organic carbon, sand, silt and clay were grouped together for each site and a cluster analysis performed, using Euclidean distance as the similarity coefficient and Ward's minimum vari-ance method as the linkage procedure to produce a dendrogram for each site, from which sediment facies and subfacies groupings were obtained. Samples for dating were taken at 0.5cm, 2cm and 1cm (Streamstown) intervals from tidal marsh edge localities adjacent to cores BBB and STB.

The samples were ashed at 550°C and the less than 63mm fraction sent to the Department of Physics, University of Bremen, sive tidal flats cut by a channel. The Ballysadare River drains a larger catchment than the Bracky River and contains several lakes.

The mean annual rainfall in the area is around 1200mm/yr. Land reclamation which occurred between 1836 and 1913 near the site may have influenced sedimentation patterns in this part of the bay. The tidal marsh is mature, existing between 1.07m and 2.19m OD, with highest elevations along the where the samples were treated and the concentra-tions of radioisotopes of 134 Cs, 137 Cs, 210 Pb and 214 Pb were determined g-spectrometrically using a Canberra 55% N-type High-Purity Germanium detector. Prior to the measurements, the samples were sealed and stored until 226 Ra was in equilibrium with its decay daughter 214 Pb. Ages were calculated from excess 210 Pb concentrations using the 'constant initial concentration model'. Correction was made for grain size and organic carbon concentration effects.

Since the primary concern was with pollution levels within the sediment, sample preparation and digestion techniques were chosen that would ex-tract heavy metals bound to all particle sizes and sediment types but not heavy metals that were an integral part of the sediment mineralogy.

Samples were pre-treated using standard methods (Bernas 1968). Atomic absorption spectrophotometry (AAS) was used to determine heavy metal concen-trations as it is the most widely used method of trace element analysis in environmental materials such as waters,. soil sediments and tissues (Aston 1985). The aqueous solutions from sample digests were analysed using the Perkin Elmer AAS 3100. A blank digest, viz. a Teflon bomb containing only acid, was analysed for every batch of samples, as well as a repeat digest for every fifth sample to test for reproducibility.

RESULTS

Core Descriptions

The lithological characteristics of the cores are presented graphically using the Troels-Smith (1955) sediment classification scheme (Figs 3 and 4) and described below. BBA (intertidal flat: 1.3m OD) consists mainly of muds, with gravel and coarse sand dominating the base. Shell fragments are present throughout to varying degrees. Black mottling is evident throughout the core.

The up-per part of BBB (tidal marsh edge: 1.5m OD) is dominated by peat and organic clay, with lower levels having a higher clastic content. Extensive root penetration and decaying vegetative matter are evident throughout. Lamination becomes more obvious with depth. BBC (supratidal: 2.56m OD) consists of humified peat, with two visible layers showing organic clay enrichment. Root penetration and decaying vegetative matter are present throughout. STA (tidal flat: 1.07m OD) consists of fine sands and silts with occasional shell fragments.

The base of the core is marked by an impenetrable gravel layer. STB (tidal marsh edge: 1.68m OD) consists of humified peat grading to organic-rich clastics at depth. There is extensive root penetra-tion and occasional sand and silty sand lenses. STC (backmarsh: 1.42m OD) possesses two alternating units of peat and organic-rich clastics resting on a silt-dominant unit at the base. Root penetration and decaying vegetative matter decrease down-wards, with lamina visible at the lower depths.

ORGANIC CARBON CONTENT

The organic carbon content for each of the cores is presented graphically (Figs 3 and 4) and described below. The organic carbon content of BBA remains relatively stable at approximately 3.7% above 0.87m OD, below which values fall to 1.5% with the exception of one point (4.6% at 0.77m OD). The organic carbon content of BBB varies between 15.8% at 1.41m OD to 6.2% at 0.89m OD, with maximum values near the top (1.41m OD) and lower levels (1.09m OD). In the supratidal zone (BBC), the organic carbon content is high (averaging 75%). Values vary from 61.4% to 93.5% between 2.56m and 2.31m OD, below which values remain at around 96%.

At Stream-stown, lower organic carbon contents were found in the tidal flat (STA). A gradual decline from 2% at 1.06m OD to 0.8% by 0.86m OD can be extrapolated. At the Streamstown tidal marsh edge (STB), values decline steadily from 19.2% at the top of the core to 3.7% at 1.56m OD, below which values remain relatively stable at around 5%. At the backmarsh (STC), the organic carbon con-tent declines from 62.5% at the top of the core to 21.5% at 1.26m OD, below which values rise to 39.6% at 0.98m OD before falling to 11.1% at the base of the core. For both sites, organic carbon content increases landward, e.g. 1% (STA) to 38% (STC) and 3% (BBA) to 86% (BBC), as a result of a decrease in clastic input and an increase in waterlogging facilitating peat formation.

GRAIN SIZE

The percentage sand, silt and clay for each of the cores are presented graphically (Figs 3 and 4) and described below. All the cores are dominated by silt. In BBA, the percentage sand increases between 1.29m and 0.97m OD, below which silt content increases at the expense of sand. This pattern mirrors variations in percentage organic carbon. Percentage sand, silt and clay values for BBB and BBC are relatively consistent throughout the cores, with variation in percentage clay in the lower part of BBC.

The tidal flat core (STA) reveals relatively consistent values throughout, with percentage clay content reaching a maximum of only 0.9% at 1.02m OD. The tidal marsh edge core (STB) shows some variation, with an increase in sand at the expense of silt at the top and bottom of the core. The supratidal core (STC) reveals a near-equal proportion of clay and sand, with values being relatively consistent throughout.

DEPOSITIONAL FACIES

Percentage values for organic carbon, sand, silt, and clay were collated for each site and grouped via cluster analysis, which produced a dendrogram for each site. The data for these den-drograms are presented in Tables 1 and 2. The depositional facies are presented graphically in Figs 3 and 4. The facies analyses for the Bracky Bridge and Streamstown sites show three distinct deposi-tional environments (tidal flat, tidal marsh edge and backmarsh/supratidal) with facies specific to each core. Facies are sometimes repeated within a core but not between cores. An exception to this is the occurrence of facies found in the tidal flat cores in both tidal marsh edge cores.

DATING

Both tidal marsh edge profiles were dated using the radioisotopes of 134 Cs, 137 Cs, 210 Pb and 214 Pb. Concentrations of 134 Cs and 137 Cs in the profiles reflect atmospheric nuclear fallout as a result of human activity and can be interpreted to provide dates corresponding to the initiation of atomic weapons testing (1954), the test ban treaty (1963) and the Chernobyl accident (1986) (Pen-nington et al. 1973; Ritchie et al. 1973; Ehlers et al. 1993). 210 Pb (t 1/2 =22 years) is produced in the atmosphere as a decay product of 222 Rn; it is rapidly attached to the atmospheric aerosol and deposited on all exposed surfaces (Sugai 1990). In the marine system, the isotope becomes bonded to suspended sediment particles. By extrapolating from the half-life curve of the isotope it is possible to produce an independent dated profile which validates the caesium interpretations and allows dating of earlier sediments (Sugai 1990). Ages were calculated assuming a constant sedimentation rate and are shown in Figs 3 and 4.

HEAVY METAL ANALYSIS

The levels (in mg of metal per kg of dry sediment) of five heavy metals-lead, copper, zinc, chromium and manganese-for each core from both sites are presented graphically in Figs 3 and 4 and described below.

BBA (tidal flat) reveals a general increase in heavy metal content from the base upwards. The exception to this is the plot for lead, which shows a peak in the middle of the profile. Copper, chromium and manganese concentrations show minimal variation. Copper concentrations reveal a steady increase from the bottom up, followed by a decline in the top

5cm of the profile. Zinc con-centrations show no clear trend, and chromium shows a peak and decline at the top of the profile. Manganese concentrations also increase at the top of the profile.

The core from the tidal marsh edge (BBB) shows a degree of variation in lead content with no clear trend. Copper concentrations show maximum values at the base and the top of the core. Con-centrations for zinc and chromium are relatively uniform, increasing upwards from probable background levels below 1.25m OD. Manganese shows a peak of 1368mg kg-1 at 1.41m OD, after which the levels fall by a factor of approximately ten and below which concentrations are more stable. In the supratidal core (BBC) lead concentrations show a slight increase upward, with a more pronounced increase between 2.44m and 2.56m OD. Copper and zinc levels show a degree of variation throughout the core, with zinc levels in the top 10cm almost double those at the base. Concentrations of both metals show an increase upwards through the core. Chromium shows ele-vated levels above 2.46m OD. Manganese concen-tration rises sharply from 28.8mg kg -1 at 2.47m OD to 129.6mg kg -1 at 2.55m OD. Below 2.47m OD manganese levels show little variation. All heavy metal concentrations from the tidal flats (STA) show relatively consistent trends, with the exception of copper levels, which decrease between 0.82m and 0.78m OD. All the other heavy metal levels show a steady decrease down-ward through the core, especially zinc.

The core from the tidal marsh edge (STB) shows a sharp increase in all metals upwards through the core, especially in the top 9cm; an exception to this is the chromium concentration, which decreases toward the top. Variation from this general pattern of decreasing metal concentrations is minimal, with the exception of copper. The backmarsh core (STC) shows a similar pattern to STB, with low, relatively uniform con-centrations rising sharply in the top 13cm of the core. However, in this case, all levels, except chromium, decrease in the top 5cm of the core.

DISCUSSION

Interpretation of Heavy Metal Concentrations

Overall, most heavy metal levels for Streams-town are higher than at Bracky Bridge. As a consequence it may be suggested that analytical error will be less amplified at Bracky Bridge, which may help to explain why the trends shown for the Streamstown cores indicate a more definite pat-tern, viz. a decrease from top to bottom of the core. Background concentrations of heavy metals are inferred from the stable, low-level values in the lower half of the profile.

The cores from Streamstown show a surficial enrichment of all metals in the uppermost 10cm which becomes increasingly pronounced landward across the marsh. Surficial enrichment and an in-crease in metal loadings landward is also evident at Bracky Bridge, albeit to a lesser extent as overall metal concentrations are lower. This is particularly true for the concentrations of copper, zinc and lead at Bracky Bridge, which are low enough to ap-proach the detection limits of the technique, mak-ing interpretations difficult.

At both sites the surficial enrichment corres-ponds to the most recent sediments (approximately the last 30 years: see Figs 3 and 4), which may suggest an increase in anthropogenic activity. The Streamstown site has a much larger catchment and may therefore receive metals from more anthropo-genic sources.

The data show an increase in organic carbon and clay content landward across the two sites. Limited variation in these parameters is expressed vertically in the cores, although spatial (landward) and vertical variation is unlikely to differ dramati-cally between the two sites owing to similarities in the depositional environments. This statement is supported by the facies analysis. Heavy metal con-centrations at the two sites should also show a certain degree of similarity in terms of their vertical and spatial attributes.

Organic carbon and clay contents are major controlling influences on the binding of heavy metals (De Groot et al. 1976; Fletcher et al. 1994; Williams et al. 1994). This can be demonstrated by correlating heavy metal concentrations with or-ganic carbon and clay content for each sample. The results for Streamstown and Bracky Bridge are shown in Tables 3 and 4. In general, correlation is stronger at Streamstown than at Bracky Bridge, possibly reflecting lower metal concentrations at the latter.

However, the degree of correlation does not totally explain the controls on heavy metal enrich-ment. For example, at BBA and BBB, lead shows maximum concentration in samples where both percentage organic carbon and percentage clay are low. The opposite is true at corresponding points in STA and STB, although they do not differ significantly in terms of facies. Other examples exist: for instance, manganese concentrations are highest in samples from BBA and BBB, where percentage organic carbon levels are low; however, in STA and STB manganese concentrations are highest when percentage organic carbon levels are high. These irregularities may again partly reflect the low heavy metal concentrations at Bracky Bridge.

Despite the fact that percentage organic car-bon and percentage clay do not completely clarify the situation regarding heavy metal distribution, organic carbon content may exert a strong influ-ence on heavy metal concentrations (Fletcher et al. 1994). In this case, for example, zinc concentration and organic carbon show a correlation of 0.942 at STA even though overall organic carbon content in the tidal flats is low. Organic matter in a sediment may also possess a higher cation exchange capacity and therefore a greater propensity to ad-sorb metals (De Groot et al. 1976). Hypotheses can be posed to explain other processes that may affect heavy metal binding.

These may include the tidal suspension and rede-position of clastic material containing bound metals from the tidal flats onto the marsh edge during tidal inundation. In tidal flats where sulphate re-duction is dominant, metal ions are more likely to be precipitated as insoluble metal sulphides which are less likely to be flushed through a sediment if the extent of water percolation through that sedi-ment is limited (Warren 1981).

These insoluble precipitates may subsequently be remobilised by tidal suspension and redeposition. This process may account for higher heavy metal concentrations at the marsh edge as opposed to the supratidal area at Bracky Bridge. At Streamstown the highest heavy metal concentrations are in the supratidal area. This may simply reflect the significantly higher sedimentation rate at the marsh edge (STB) at Streamstown.

As well as physical influences, certain physico-chemical processes may be in action. For example, some metals, such as zinc and chromium, form strong complexes with chloride ligands and there-fore changes in salinity may have profound effects on their solubility (Förstner and Salomons 1980). In fact, chromium concentrations at Streamstown show enrichment in the top 5cm of the supratidal area but a decrease in the top 9cm of the marsh edge.

The formation of a chromium-chloride complex, which is less stable than a chromium-humic acid complex present in the supratidal marsh, would facilitate greater mobility of chromium in this area of frequent inundation where changes in salinity are common. This theory is supported by the lower correlation shown be-tween chromium and clay and organic carbon content at the marsh edge.

Another physico-chemical process may be ex-pressed by the manganese concentrations, which are lowest in the supratidal areas for both sites, with the tidal flat concentrations being greater than those of the tidal marsh edge (with the exception of an enrichment in the upper 9cm). In the supratidal setting, water-table fluctuations facilitate changes in redox conditions in the upper levels of the profile, with relatively high freshwater input, owing to the high rainfall, reducing salinity. Manganese oxides are reduced in anoxic sediments to the more soluble Mn 2+ form, which can enter the interstitial waters of the sediment (Beeftink and Rozema 1988).

The anoxic conditions present in the tidal flats may facilitate the reduction of man-ganese oxides but the amount of percolation oc-curring may be too low to facilitate any substantial manganese removal. However, in the supratidal setting, with the increased freshwater input, re-moval may occur. Furthermore, the manganese enrichment seen in the younger sediments of all cores may be partly re-precipitated Mn 2+, pre-sumably in the form of insoluble oxyhydroxides, diffusing to the surface. A similar transient storage of manganese and higher concentrations in surface layers has been demonstrated in other tidal marshes (McCaffrey and Thompson 1980). Certain metal ions, including manganese, have been shown to exhibit elevated concentrations in interstitial waters (Duchart et al. 1973).

In tidal marshes redox condi-tions will fluctuate with varying water-levels, resulting in different usage of electron acceptors, and therefore different ions will be released to the interstitial waters (Beeftink and Rozema 1988). The fact that manganese concentrations at these sites are high compared to background concentra-tions could suggest that two processes may be affecting the heavy metal distribution in near-sur-face sediments: i.e., in addition to the possibility of diagenetic mobilisation of manganese in response to changes in redox potential, we may also find an increased anthropogenic input.

Of the five metals analysed in the samples from Bracky Bridge, vertical variation in concen-tration in the lower 40-45cm for chromium, manganese and zinc appears to represent back-ground concentrations. The fluctuation of lead and copper suggests that the background concentra-tions for these metals are approaching the detection limits of the technique.

THE ANTHROPOGENIC INPUT OF HEAVY METALS TO THE STUDY SITE

It is difficult to make a quantitative estimate of the anthropogenic input of heavy metals into an environment since no direct evidence exists con-cerning the heavy metal content of the sediment from the pre-industrial periods (De Groot et al. 1976). It is also impractical to monitor all potential sources of contamination within a catchment.

The extent of anthropogenic heavy metal pollution in a tidal marsh environment will depend, amongst other factors, on the nature of the discharge into the catchments of the estuary. Within the catch-ment area of Bracky Bridge, the only sizeable settlement is Ardara. The dominant industry within the catchment is agriculture, mainly sheep-farming, although there are some small firms involved in wool-dyeing and weaving in Ardara itself.

The area receives many seasonal visitors, especially during the summer. The mountainous catchment has fairly poor soils drained by a plethora of streams. With no intensive agriculture or heavy industry, we can assume that the main source of pollution will be from sewage, with some input of effluent from the wool-dyeing businesses. The catchment of the Streamstown site covers a much larger area, with Ballysadare and Collooney being the two major settlements.

The N4 and N17 are busy roads, being the main route for road traffic to the south and west of Ireland from the north-west of Ireland and western parts of Northern Ireland.

Agriculture is again the main industry in this catchment but with intensive arable and dairy farming being the dominant forms. The volume of agricultural effluent would be much greater in this area owing to the size of the catchment and the type of farming carried out. Ballysadare town has a salmon and trout hatchery on the banks of the Ballysadare River near the site of an old flour mill which closed down fifteen years ago.

There is also a disused lead mine at Abbey-town. There is no heavy industry in the area so the main effluent inputs to the system will be agricultural, domestic waste effluent and the effluent from the fish hatcheries. Another source of pollution may be the nearby large town of Sligo, where there is some industry. Dredging of Sligo harbour may remobilise heavy metals, which may then find their way into the Ballysadare Bay system.

To assess the anthropogenic heavy metal input one must determine background levels of heavy metals with which to compare our observed levels. These can be approximated from sediments of 'pre-industrial' age. The term 'pre-industrial' refers here to those deposits laid down before any form of large-scale industry or population pressure appeared in the west of Ireland. We have arbitrarily taken this to mean pre-1950, although at Bracky Bridge it could be argued that the area is still pre-industrial.

Radiometric dating implies that 'pre-industrial' lev-els exist below 1.26m OD at BBB, and at STB the whole core is 'post-industrial'. Facies analysis has classified identical sediment types at both 'pre-industrial' and 'post-industrial' levels in BBB and probably all cores from Bracky Bridge. In all cases, heavy metal concentrations are higher near the top of the cores in 'post-industrial' facies. From this, taking account of other factors affecting the con-centration of heavy metals, we can conclude that there is probably a degree of anthropogenic input to the two sites, especially during the last 25 years.

It could be argued that EEC agricultural and rural tourism policies have contributed to an increase in anthropogenic activity, and hence have increased the potential for increased sewage effluent, in this area. However, the low levels found suggest that the coastal environment of the north-west coast of Ireland is still relatively clean, and consequently the potential for ecotoxicological damage to the site is also minimal.

At Streamstown, anthropogenic inputs are higher. For instance, increased levels of lead may be a result of increased inputs of tetraethyl lead as a direct consequence of the much higher volume of motor traffic that would pass through the terrestrial catchment of the Streamstown site, entering the catchment via road run-off. The vertical fluctuation is much lower in the samples from Streamstown than in those from Bracky Bridge. This may sup-port the suggestion that the levels of lead at Bracky Bridge were indeed close to the detection levels of the technique.

CONCLUSION

In conclusion, it may be stated that the level of heavy metals found in both tidal marshes is low, supporting the accepted view that the north-west coast of Ireland presents a comparatively clean environment. Indeed, it may be argued that these sites are examples of pristine sites, with probably no ecotoxicological effects on tidal marsh flora and fauna at present.

However, many variables are responsible for controlling the occurrence and spa-tial distribution of heavy metal pollutants, making each tidal marsh case specific. On this basis, the data presented do not dismiss the possibility that pollution hotspots may exist in other locations along the west coast.

The complexities of diagenesis suggest that no clear conclusions should be drawn regarding the nature of heavy metal biogeochemistry or the source of the anthropogenic inputs in these tidal marshes in north-west Ireland. Heavy metal levels at Bracky Bridge were slightly lower than at Streamstown, probably reflecting increased anthro-pogenic activity in the Streamstown catchment. Both sites show a spatial variation in the heavy metal content of the sediments, with greater con-centrations found further inland. This is a conse-quence of increased organic content inland and a tendency towards peat development. Organogenic tidal marshes are a feature of the west coast of Ireland, and if pollution were to become severe these tidal marshes could become pollution sinks. Both tidal marshes show evidence of enrich-ment in the upper levels, starting at around 1970.

7

The Fight Against Highly Toxic Mercury in the Environment

The late singer-songwriter Laura Nyro loved to eat tuna fish. An avid environmentalist, she was shocked to hear that her favorite food was contaminated with the toxic heavy metal mercury, and she expressed her anger in a song. "I'm young enough, I'm old enough in the city machine/Where industries fill the fish full of mercury (it's tax free)."

Nyro was right to worry about eating fish, and right about industrial mercury use. Forty states have issued advisories about eating fish that may have high levels of mercury in their tissues. As recently as last July, Massachusetts public health officials warned young women and children under 12 to stop eating "most" fish caught in state rivers and lakes, and to avoid certain seafood. Tuna was on the list, as was swordfish.

Mercury is a persistent heavy metal, processed into a liquid from mined cinnabar, that accumulates in water and in the tissues of humans, fish and animals. It was declared a hazardous air pollutant by the Environmental Protection Agency (EPA) in 1971. According to the federal Agency for Toxic Substances and Disease Registry, long-term human exposure to mercury in either organic or inorganic form "can permanently damage the brain, kidneys, and developing fetuses." A potent neurotoxin, mercury is slowly being phased out of many commercial uses, including consumer thermometers, but it is still used in many industrial processes and is in such products as fluorescent lights, home and appliance thermostats, and even toys.

Ask most people about mercury in the environment and they're apt to think of broken thermometers. But the truth is that industry, in the form of coal-fired power plants, electric arc furnaces (which melt and recycle the steel from old cars) and municipal waste incinerators are the major sources.

In landfills and in water, bacterial contamination turns mercury into its most toxic form, methyl mercury. Mercury also gets into the environment in pharmaceutical products, and through ritual religious uses, especially in Latin American Santeria (see sidebar). Mercury sells for less than $2 a pound on the wholesale market, and even when it is "recycled," it may still end up in the environment.

Progress is being made to end some of mercury's more visible uses, but the campaign is far from over. Five states have laws that either put some restrictions on mercury use, sale or disposal or require labeling of products containing it. Similar bills are pending in 15 state legislatures. "Despite state and local bans, thousands of retailers still sell mercury thermometers to consumers who aren't aware of the risks," says Felice Stadler, policy coordinator of the National Wildlife Federation's Clean the Rain campaign.

"Just one seventieth of a teaspoon of atmospheric mercury can contaminate a 20-acre lake for a year," says Michael Bender, executive director of the Vermont-based Mercury Policy Project. "We have to take mercury permanently out of commerce. It's not that difficult to containerize it and store it indefinitely. An ideal solution would be the kind of 'producer responsibility' laws they have in Europe, which make companies responsible for their waste."

U.S. Senator Susan Collins (R-ME) has proposed legislation that would create a task force to address the mercury problem on a national scale. Under her bill, the Mercury Reduction and Disposal Act, S.351, the sale of thermometers containing the metal would be banned nationally, and the mercury inside them would be stockpiled and treated similarly to nuclear waste. Stadler says, "Enacting a nationwide ban on sales is essential."

In response to a campaign led by Health Care Without Harm (HCWH), five drugstore chains, including CVS, Rite-Aid, Walgreens, Wal-Mart and Eckerd, have agreed to stop selling mercury thermometers.

These companies represent 71 percent of chain pharmacies, but mercury thermometers are still on sale at Kroger, Medicine Shoppe, Publix and Fred's stores. "It's appalling that there are retailers that continue to sell potentially dangerous mercury devices to their customers, especially when safe alternatives exist in the marketplace," says Jamie Harvie, mercury coordinator of HCWH. Eight states and a number of cities have banned or restricted the sale of mercury thermometers, and 600 hospitals and clinics have agreed to get mercury out of their waste streams.

But mercury thermometers are only one, very visible part of the problem. Because mercury has many uses and applications, the movement to get it out of the atmosphere must take a multi-pronged approach. Some of the campaigns have made more headway than others, but all have acquired a new urgency as the dangers of mercury become better known.

FISH FILLED WITH MERCURY

According to a 2001 Centers for Disease Control and Prevention (CDC) study, one of 10 American women of childbearing age is at risk for having a baby born with neurological problems due to in utero mercury exposure. Statistically, that means 375,000 babies are at risk every year. Nearly six million women who might be considering having a child already have mercury levels above EPA safety guidelines.

As recounted in Morbidity and Mortality Weekly Report, the CDC study was based on a national survey of mercury in blood and hair, while previous studies were estimates based on per capita fish consumption. "New studies show that far more women are at risk of exposure to methyl mercury than previously thought," says Caroline Smith DeWaal, director of food safety at the Center for Science in the Public Interest. She urges the Food and Drug Administration (FDA) to monitor commercial seafood and to remove unsafe fish from the market.

A federal General Accounting Office (GAO) report, commissioned by Senator Tom Harkin (D-IA) in 1999, concludes that the FDA has failed in its efforts to protect the public from mercury-tainted seafood.

The report faulted the FDA's Hazard Analysis Critical Point regulations for not providing proper guidance to the fishing industry about safeguarding the public.

A joint report by the Mercury Policy Project and California Communities Against Toxics in 2000 charged that the FDA had stopped mercury monitoring for tuna, shark and swordfish, despite the fact that the FDA's previous testing found more than one part per million (considered the "action level") of mercury in more than half the swordfish it evaluated.

Some 33 percent of shark tissue studied by the FDA was found to exceed the action level for mercury, as was four percent of tuna. In 2001, the FDA finally recommended that women of childbearing age not eat shark, swordfish, king mackerel or tilefish. Tuna was not mentioned.

"The GAO report shows that mercury pollution threatens both sportfish and seafood," says Eric Uram of the Sierra Club's Midwestern office. "Consumers need to watch what fish they eat, no matter where it comes from--the restaurant, store, lake or seashore."

A 2001 study that looked specifically at the New England states gave them a mixed report card for their efforts to reduce mercury levels in the environment, and warn the public about the risks.

The New England Zero Mercury Campaign praised the states for developing health-based advisories about mercury in fish, but it urged them to do more to "effectively communicate these health warnings to women who may become pregnant and families with young children--.Strategically targeted and culturally sensitive outreach and education is needed to prevent dangerous mercury exposure from fish, especially from commonly eaten seafood."

Prenatal mercury exposure, said the New England report, "can hurt children's ability to remember, pay attention, talk, draw, run and play, and increase the number of children who have trouble keeping up in school or require special education, according to the National Academy of Sciences."

According to Dr. Ted Schettler of Physicians for Social Responsibility, "Relatively small amounts of contaminated fish eaten often, or larger amounts eaten occasionally, can harm developing fetal brains during windows of vulnerability. The fetus is extremely sensitive to mercury."

SWITCHING OFF AUTO MERCURY

What do the high-intensity headlights, anti-lock brake systems, global positioning screens and trunk-or hood-mounted light switches on your car have in common? They all may contain highly toxic mercury.

The Clean Car Campaign, a coalition of several environmental groups, is trying to persuade the auto industry to not only stop all uses of mercury, but also to take responsibility for the heavy metal already installed in hundreds of millions of on-the-road vehicles.

The industry has agreed to phase out most uses of mercury switches by the end of the 2001 model year, but it is not surprisingly balking at the monumental effort needed to remove existing switches, many of which it says would prove difficult to locate. (At presstime, the state of Maine passed landmark legislation requiring carmakers to pay for a mercury auto switch recovery program that will take at least 90 pounds of the metal out of the environment every year.)

According to the Mercury Policy Project's Bender, the auto industry installed 10 tons of mercury in car switches in 1995, although that amount was dramatically reduced by the 2001 model year. Mercury light switches are now used in only a few General Motors vehicles. Most European and Japanese auto manufacturers stopped installing mercury convenience light switches in the mid-1990s. But even as the switches are being phased out, many domestic and foreign companies are equipping their cars with headlights, brake components and navigational systems containing mercury.

The EPA, in a report to Congress in 1997, estimated that 158 tons of the metal are released into the atmosphere annually from manmade sources in the U.S. "The auto industry is not the major source, but it's definitely a significant source," says Bender, who points to coal-fired power plants and waste combustors as the prime culprits nationally for mercury release.

Charles Griffith, the auto project director of Michigan's Ecology Center, a member of the Clean Car Campaign, says that the mercury in auto switches is released into the atmosphere when steel recovered from scrapped automobiles is melted down in electric arc furnaces (EAFs). A study produced jointly by the Ecology Center, the Buffalo-based Great Lakes United and the University of Tennessee Center for Clean Products and Clean Technologies estimates that 15.6 metric tons of mercury are released annually by EAFs, more than all other manufacturing sources combined.

Bob Kainz, a senior manager for pollution prevention and life cycle programs at DaimlerChrysler, says that only two of the company's 2001 products, the Jeep Cherokee and Wrangler, still had mercury switches in their ABS brake systems, and that both models will be free of the heavy metal when they're redesigned over the next few years.

"There are better ways of handling this problem than going after the carmakers," Kainz says. "Eighty-seven percent of the mercury going out into the atmosphere is coming from utility boilers, waste combustors, coal-fired power plants, cement plants and medical incinerators." Kainz adds that DaimlerChrysler's records do not consistently identify which cars or trucks actually have mercury switches.

The auto industry, through such trade groups as the Alliance of Automobile Manufacturers and the Association of International Automobile Manufacturers, has lobbied against the laws, arguing that it is phasing out mercury on its own. Greg Dana, vice president for environmental affairs of the Alliance of Automobile Manufacturers, says that General Motors, Ford and DaimlerChrysler began removing mercury from their products in 1995 under an agreement with the state of Michigan. The mercury switches in existing cars, he says, should be removed when the car is at the end of its life. "The recyclers are already taking out the gasoline, oil, and air-conditioner refrigerant," Dana says. "It's a simple add-on for them to rip out the mercury switches."

The auto trade groups support legislation requiring recyclers to remove the switches as part of the dismantling process, but this has produced a fierce reaction from junkyard operators and scrap steel dealers. Both the Automotive Recyclers Association (ARA) and the Institute of Scrap Recycling Industries say they have little financial incentive to take on the task, with each switch containing only a gram of the metal and mercury trading at less than $2 a pound.

According to ARA Vice President Bill Steinkuller, "The auto manufacturers engineered the vehicles to include mercury switches, produced the product and profited from it. From our point of view, it defies logic that they now want to deny any responsibility for the mercury and put the onus on the dismantlers."

The auto industry and the recyclers are fighting a war of words over mercury, but there is some chance of reconciliation. "We're not trying to pick a fight with the manufacturers," Steinkuller says. "If we get beyond the rhetoric, we can probably get together and handle this problem." Unfortunately, ARA's proposed solution--in which the carmakers foot the bill for a nationwide program of mercury collection and storage--is precisely the kind of high-cost program the auto industry is trying to avoid.

CHEWING ON MERCURY

Anita Vasquez Tibau was a young college dance major 20 years ago when she suddenly found herself unable to breathe. "I could hardly walk," she told Dr. L.A. McKeown in an article for WebMD Medical News. "I couldn't do anything. I was using my inhaler every half hour." These problems plagued Tibau for 20 years until, in 2000, a blood test showed she was highly sensitive to mercury. After Tibau had a dentist remove all 13 of her mercury fillings, her health improved dramatically. She no longer uses any asthma medicine, and she reports much higher energy levels and an increased attention span.

The American Dental Association (ADA) reports that 76 percent of dentists use dental amalgam--a mixture of metals, including silver, dissolved with mercury. The ADA denies that there are any safety problems with dental amalgam. "Studies have failed to find any link between amalgam restorations and any medical disorder," the association says. But it concedes that "a very small number of people" are allergic to the fillings. "Fewer than 100 cases have ever been reported," says the ADA. "Symptoms of amalgam allergy are very similar to a typical skin allergy."

The ADA defended its position in court last year after Consumers for Dental Choice sued the ADA and the California Dental Association, claiming that both groups were misleading the public about the mercury content of what they call "silver fillings." But the ADA says it has never tried to hide the mercury connection.

A paper prepared by Consumers for Dental Choice and DAMS, another anti-amalgam advocacy group, charges that every amalgam filling releases 10 micrograms of mercury into the body daily, which is two-thirds of the excretable mercury level. The report also charges that mercury can cross the placental barrier into the tissue of a developing fetus, and it implicates the metal in kidney impairment, loss of immune function, antibiotic resistance and lowered fertility.

Boyd Haley, chairman of the chemistry department at the University of Kentucky, has been an expert witness before Congress on the mercury issue. "They place this stuff in people's mouths and it's toxic before it goes in, and it's toxic when it is placed in your tooth, so how does it suddenly become safe?" he asks. Many dentists, under pressure on the mercury issue, have switched to alternatives. According to Richard Epstein, a Connecticut-based dentist, "While I believe that the studies disparaging silver amalgam are seriously flawed, the alternatives are effective enough to warrant switching. I now use gold and composite materials."

Dentists have also been under fire for releasing unused amalgam into the waste stream, where it can enter the aquatic food chain. Some have invested in disposable amalgam traps, which catch the metal before it goes down the drain. Recaptured amalgam can be shipped to groups like Dental Recycling North America, which recovers 90 to 95 percent of the mercury in the fillings.

Congresswoman Diane Watson (D-CA) introduced legislation last year that would ban all mercury-based dental amalgam in five years. The New York State Dental Association has fought a proposed bill that would, among other things, require dentists to use mercury containment traps, file an annual amalgam report, and no longer use the fillings for pregnant or under-15-year-old patients. The association claims the legislation is "misguided" and "would detrimentally alter the practice of dentistry."

FROM THE SMOKESTACK

According to the National Academy of Sciences (NAS), dirty power plants, especially those that burn coal (which contains mercury naturally), are the single largest source of mercury emissions, resulting in an estimated 40 tons a year. Eighty-five percent of all mercury pollution in the U.S. is released either by coal plants or municipal and medical waste incinerators burning mercury-tainted trash. Only the incinerator emissions are regulated.

In 2000, a NAS report urged that mercury releases from power plants be drastically curtailed. Before leaving office, the Clinton Administration announced that it would develop new, stricter standards, to be proposed in 2003 and finalized in 2004. Then-EPA Administrator Carol Browner noted, "The greatest source of mercury emissions is power plants, and they have never been required to control these emissions before now."

Upon taking office, the Bush Administration signaled that it might reverse campaign promises about power plant carbon dioxide and mercury emissions. The move came after heavy industry pressure from the Utility Air Regulatory Group, which represents 50 large power plants.

Environmentalists loudly protested the administration's proposed reversal. "Countless studies have documented that mercury emissions from U.S. sources, including coal-fired electric utilities, contaminate lakes and streams, the fish within those water bodies, and the people and wildlife who eat the fish," said National Wildlife Federation Senior Scientist Mike Murray.

In April 2001, the Bush Administration again changed course, attempting to quash an Edison Electric Institute lawsuit aimed at the Clinton-era mercury rules. Environmentalists were cautiously optimistic, but Bush's EPA is likely to phase in smaller mercury reductions over a longer period of time.

In model legislation created by the Mercury Policy Project, coal-burning electric utilities would be required to reduce their mercury releases 95 percent by 2008, but the Bush Administration is likely to impose a much weaker standard. Groundbreaking legislation is instead coming from the states, including Vermont, which passed the Mercury Reduction Act in 1998. That bill requires manufacturers of "mercury-added" products to label them as such when sold to the public. The legislation also banned trash disposal of products containing mercury. Vermont's bill prompted a lawsuit by fluorescent lamp manufacturers, who claimed an undue financial burden and argued that their First Amendment right not to disclose information had been violated. The lawsuit was later thrown out by two federal appeals courts.

Several other states intend to model legislation on Vermont's law. In 2001, Massachusetts unveiled strict new final standards for power plant emissions, becoming the first state in the nation to regulate mercury releases. The state's power plants will be required to phase in 50 to 75 percent nitrogen oxide and sulfur dioxide emission reductions by 2008. "From a national perspective, this mandatory reduction of four major pollutants from the state's oldest and dirtiest power plants is a very important precedent," says Cindy Luppi, organizing director of Clean Water Action.

One final irony is that U.S. campaigners may be very successful in removing mercury from domestic commerce, only to see the deadly neurotoxin "recycled" to ready buyers overseas. That was exactly the case last year, when HoltraChem, a mercury-based chlor-alkali plant in Maine, shut down. Some 130 tons of mercury were sold to a broker, which resold it for use in India. Madhumita Dutta, coordinator of the Indian group Toxics Link, calls this kind of transaction "toxic trade." Vehement protests in both India and the U.S. succeeded in at least temporarily stopping the deal, but there is an estimated 3.5 to five million pounds of mercury on-site at 11 other American chlor-alkali plants.

For environmentalists, the battle against mercury has many fronts. It's not just in thermometers, but also in pharmaceutical products and vaccines (in the form of thimerosal, a preservative), and it is in car parts, too. As soon as legislation is passed to take it out of some consumer products, it pops up in others.

A worrisome new use is in high-tech gadgetry, like global positioning screens and high-density auto headlights. Mercury pours out of smokestacks and arc furnaces and, according to the National Center for Atmospheric Research, tons of it (stored in foliage and ground litter) goes up in smoke during wildfires. It's an elusive enemy, but one well worth fighting.

8

RESEARCH INTO HEAVY METAL CONCENTRATIONS IN AGRICULTURAL SOILS

INTRODUCTION

Presently, large swine-breeding farms are gaining in popularity, as well as poultry farms are expanding in Lithuania. The sea-sonality of production and crop rotation have influence on the formation of plant cultivation waste. In addition, the plant cul-tivation waste boasts a wider application and is mainly used as fodder.It is less harmful and does not cause greater environmen-tal problems, therefore, under our country's conditions, when evaluating the real potential of biogas production, it is recom-mended to focus major attention to animal breeding farms,first of all, swine-breeding complexes (Duris, 1997).

However, there emerges a very complicated situation when fields,being in close proximity to swine-breeding farms, are fertilized by various mineral fertilizers, while liquid swine waste from these farms is used for additional fertilization of these fields, which at the same time increases pollution with heavy metals.Large amounts of sewage having unpleasant smell accumulate.

The application of liquid animal waste onto the soil results in the formation of excess nutrients, part of the sewage might reach underground waters, higher pollution has a significant effect on ecosystems and via them on humans (Ebadi et al.,2005).

With Lithuania's integration into the European Union, environmental requirements to activity objects change. Since 1 January 2004, Procedure of Issuing Permits for Natural Resource Use and Setting the Limits of Natural Resource Use and Norms of Permissible Emissions was replaced by the imple-mented System of Integrated Pollution Prevention and Control Permits (IPPC). The aim of this system is to pass over from the unified environmental requirements applied by an enterprise to the setting of individual requirements for particular equip-ment. According to IPPC rules, the conditions of permits for Appendix 1.Facilities must be based on the concept of"the best available techniques",therefore,it is necessary to analyze the best available techniques of large objects that are potentially the big-gest polluters in the animal husbandry sector (Ure,1996).

The swine breeding sector,to be more widely analyzed in this paper,is characterized by big environmental pollution (emissions into the atmosphere, water, soil) (Voronkiene et al., 2001). Many swine breeding farms in Lithuania dilute accumulated liquid ani-mal waste with water and outpour it onto the soil.Therefore,it is necessary to analyze the impact of this pollutant on the environment and determine which technologies are most suitable for this sector to reach a high level of environmental quality.

There are many land plots which are polluted with heavy metals one way or another. This pollution might cause significant adverse effects such as damage to eco-systems, change in soil quality and respective reduction of its use for farming,pol-lution of underground water layers, and harm to both human and animal health.

Agriculture is one of the main sources of pollution with heavy metals. Soil fertilization with manure is still one of the most frequently used technical means in Lithuania. Manure is considered to be a good fertilizer but when used in big amounts to enhance soil fertility it becomes one of the main sources of pollution with heavy metals in agriculture (Hutchinson,2003). The Balciunai farm, in compliance with the JSC System re-quirements, was selected for the experimental research. Its de-sign production volume amounts to 48,000 pigs per year. The complex is located near Pilviškiai town,Vilkaviškis district. After signing contracts with local farmers, the liquid swine waste is outpoured onto the fieldsfromAprilthroughNovember.

Research into heavy metal concentrations in agricultural soils Prior to outpouring it onto the soil the waste is diluted with wa-ter, mixed well by supplying air to the accumulated liquid, the amount of sewage in this liquid accounts to about 5-7%.

The liquid fertilizer is applied on the soil surface every fort-night, approximately. In our case the liquid animal waste is ap-plied on the area of roughly 2,000 ha. The main portion of the fertilized land is comprised of meadows, while the remaining part is used for growing agricultural cultures.

Since it is common knowledge that swine fodder additives contain a lot of heavy metals,and the use of liquid animal waste for fertilizing results in the excess concentrations of heavy met-als in the soil,while the rates of these concentrations are set pur-suant to the Directive 91/676/ EEC,it was decided to examine the soil pollution with heavy metals that are most often discovered in the liquid swine waste,namely,Cu,Zn,Ni,Cr and Pb.Another reason of research into pollution with heavy metals is that re-search seeking to determine this pollution of land used for agri-cultural purpose is very scarce (Ebadi et al.,2005).

The main aims of the paper are: to determine the distribution of heavy metals concentrations in the soil fertilized with the liquid swine waste; dependence of metal concentrations on different depths of the soil; dependence of metal concentration on the time elapsed from the waste application on soil surface; dependence of changes in metal concentration on the season of the year; to evaluate how the company complies with the pollu-tion criteria for IPPC permits.

MATERIALS AND METHODS

The experimental research of heavy metals was performed on the land plot of 30 ha area,used as a pasture,having even surface, covered with low grass,the prevailing type of the soil being mid-dle size loam. The field is not far from the Vilkaviškis-Pilviškiai road,from another side borders a forest and a land reclamation ditch.This area was selected for the research because due to the land reclamation ditch located on the edge of the area the excess humidity (precipitation, spilt liquid swine waste etc.) seeps to-wards the ditch, which might precondition the change of heavy metal concentrations, and the road going nearby the area may serve as a secondary source of heavy metals in this field.

The researched field was divided into 9 parts of 3.3 ha area each, and samples were taken from 16 points. The researched field has a square form,distance among researched points is 180 meters.

Samples were taken by stainless steel scoops,put into plastic bags and delivered to the laboratory. The mass of the samples amounted to 0.6-0.8 kg.Prevalent soil was rich loam. At all the 16 selected points samples were taken at two soil depths:0-10 cm and 10-20 cm.Each sample was taken using the envelope principle. Fig.1 shows the layout of sampling points. Samples were taken at different times elapsed from the liquid swine waste outpouring onto the soil:1 day after,7days after and 14 days after,prior to repeating waste application.

Soil samples were taken during different seasons of the year when the liquid swine waste was outpoured onto the fields: in spring (1-14 April), summer (1-14 June), autumn (1-14 October) (Lapinskiene et al., 2003). The experimental research was carried out at the Lithuanian University of Agriculture, Laboratory of Agrochemical Research.

Determination of heavy metals concentration. Analysis of heavy metals was performed by the atomic absorptive spec-troscopy (AAS) method. 10 grams of soil were dried at 105 °C temperature for 2 hours. After drying the sample was sieved through the sieve of 1 mm diameter meshes, afterwards dried at 105 °C temperature for 30 minutes.Then the weighted sample was put into a plastic package, later 0.5-1.0 ml. of distilled wa-ter and 21 ml of concentrated HCl and 7 ml HNO_3 acid solution were added to it. The samples were mineralized following the methods setting the required temperature and time, which are approved by the European Union and applicable in Lithuania. Upon completion of mineralization, the sample was taken out and cooled to 50-70 °C temperature.

Then solution from the vessel was filtered through a glass strainer to vessels of 50 ml each. The vessel was washed by 5 ml of diluted HNO_3 (1 : 1),and after-wards by 5 ml of distilled water. These liquids used for washing were also filtered through the glass strainer.Upon completion of the filtering the vessel was supplemented by distilled water up to the mark. Next, the concentrations of metals were determined using Buck Scientific 210VGP spectrometer with an air-acety-lene flame.If the organic partin the sample contentisbig,10-20 grams of the sample have to be put into a porcelain vessel and burnt at 450 °C temperature for 12 hours.Afterwards 1.0-1.5 g of the soil undergo mineralization with "royal live water"accord-ing to the previously described methods (Sabiene et al.,2004). Concentration is calculated according to the following for-mula: W(Me) = (C Me · f · V)

/ W, (1) where W(Me) is metal concentration,mg/kg; C Me is metal con-centration in solution, mg/l; f is dilution factor; V is volume, l (0.05 l taken for research); W is sample mass, kg, recalculated for the mass of a dry sample.

RESULTS

The maximum permissible concentrations of heavy metals are set in the hygiene standard HN 60 : 2004. This standard (HN 60 : 2004) sets the maximum permissible concentrations for the metals Cu,Cr and Pb,which is 100 mg/kg for each,Zn -300 mg/ kg and Ni -75 mg/kg.

Figures 2-4 show the dependences of Cu, Cr and Pb concentrations for the season of the year,at 0-10 cm soil depths,at different times of applying the liquid swine waste onto the soil.

One day after the waste application,Cu amount exceeds the standard by 1.1-1.7 times.Cu concentration is 1.4 times higher in autumn than in spring. Cr and Pb concentrations do not ex-ceed the values established by the standard, but in autumn the concentrations of these metals are higher by 1.3 and 1.6 times, respectively.

7 days after applying the liquid swine waste onto the soil surface, Cu amount at the depth of 10-20 cm does not exceed the set standards, while at the depth of 0-10 cm it reaches the norm only in autumn.Cu shows 1.8 times higher concentration in autumn than in spring. Cr and Pb concentrations are lower than the values established by the standard but, like in the first case,the concentrations of these metals are higher by 1.3 and 1.6 times,respectively,in autumn than in spring.

14 days after the outpouring, none of the metals show con-centrations reaching permissible standard values. During the autumn season copper concentration is 3.7 times higher than in spring.The dependence of Cr and Pb concentrations

on the sea-son of the year remains the same and is 1.3 and 1.6 times higher, respectively.

In spring Cu, Cr and Pb concentrations are the lowest, while in autumn the highest. This can lead us to the conclusion that metals are accumulating in soil. Analysis of the experiment findings shows that metal concentrations distribute nearly equally within the entire re-searched area,except for the left side of the field where the land reclamation ditch is situated.Research findings vary from 158.5 to 179.4 mg/kg.

The decrease in Cu concentration by the land reclamation ditch is around 10%,measuring point section M1-M13. It can be assumed that the decrease in heavy metal con-centration by the land reclamation ditch was recorded due to the fact that when collecting excess humidity from the researched field the amount of flowing water increases and at the same time large amounts of metals are washed out of the soil.

All the experimental findings confirm that the highest con-centrations are during the first days after the liquid swine waste application onto the soil surface,and later they are decreasing. Depending on the time of application, from 1 to 14 days, the copper concentration decreases, on average, by 7.1 times at the soil depth of 0-10 cm, and around 8.5 times when the sampling ismadeatthedepthof 10-20 cm, by 5.5 and 6.4 times in summer and 2.7 and 2.9 times in autumn, respectively.

Depending on the time of outpouring, from 1 to 14 days, Cr concentration decreas-es, on average, 1.2 times at both researched soil depths in spring and summer,and 1.3 times at both researched depths in autumn. Dependingonthetimeof outpouring, from 1to14days,leadcon-centration decreases, on average, 1.6 times at the depth of 0-10 cm and around 1.5 times at the depth of 10-20 cm in spring, 1.5 times in summer and 1.7 times autumnat both depths.

Research into heavy metal concentrations in agricultural soils Since the concentrations of heavy metals depend on the soil depth, the obtained results show that copper concentration in the upper sampling layer is 13.4-23.5% higher than that de-termined in the second layer,the concentration of chromium is 5-7.1% and that of lead is 8.4-11.7%.

Theresearchshowsthatleadconcentrationintheresearched area has higher values by the neighbouring road.At the measur-ing points (in the section) M13-M16 lead concentrations by the road Vilkaviškis-Marijampole increase, on average, by 9%. This shows that intensive traffic flows cause pollution. Figures 5,6 display the dependence of zinc and nickel con-centrations on the season of the year at the soil sampling depth of 0-10 cm and on different time from outpouring the liquid swine waste onto the soil surface.

At the soil depth of 0-10 cm zinc concentrations exceed the permissible norms only in autumn and this makes up 1.1 times after 1 day of outpouring. In autumn zinc concentration is 1.9 times bigger than in spring. The determined concentrations on nickel were regularly below the permissible limit and increased 1.7 times compared to those in spring.

At the soil depth of 10-20 cm zinc concentrations exceed the permissible norms only in autumn one day after outpouring the liquid swine waste onto the field showing the increase of 1.1 times. In autumn zinc concentration is 1.9 times bigger than in spring.In all the researched cases nickel concentrations are low-er than the permissible ones,and an increase in concentration is 1.6 times comparing the autumn and spring seasons. Like in previous cases,it was determined that zinc concentra-tions are the lowest in spring and afterwards gradually increase showing the highest concentrations of heavy metals in autumn. This once again proves the fact that a regular application of the liquid animal waste onto the soil results in the accumulation of metals in the soil.

Change in nickel concentration preserves the same tendencies, and the maximum concentrations at both researched depths of the soil do not exceed the maximum standard rates applicable in Lithuania.

The experimental research determined maximum values of zinc concentration during the autumn season of liquid animal waste application, which change from 290 to 332.5 mg/kg. the estimated value is 10-15% higher than the one in research re-sults by others foreign scientists (Chen, Lee 1997; Liu et al., 1998).The analysis of research findings shows that zinc concen-trations by the land reclamation ditch fall, on average, by 8%.

The research findings once again prove that the maximum con-centrations of heavy metals are recorded during the first days after the liquid animal waste outpouring onto the soil and they are gradually decreasing until the next outpouring,however,due to intensive application of the waste,every 14 days,the accumu-lation of these metals has been observed in the soil. Depending on the time elapsed from the liquid animal waste application,in the period from 1 to 14 days,zinc concentration, on average, decreases 2.2 times at the depth of 2-10 cm and around 2.6 times at the soil depth of 10-20 cm, by 2.8 and 3.2 times in summer,and 2.3 and 2.4 times in autumn,respectively. In the period from 1 to 14 days afterthewasteapplication,nickel concentrations decrease, on average, 1.7 times at the soil depth of 0-10 cm,and 1.8 times at the soil depth of 10-20 in the spring season, and 1.9 times in summer and 1.5 times in autumn at both researched soil depths.

Analysis of the heavy metals in question shows that the ten-dency of changes of heavy metal concentrations depends on the soil sampling depth.It is obtained that zinc concentration is 2-3.6% lower in the lower level of the researched soil 1 day after the waste application.When more days pass from the waste ap-plication this tendency becomes even more obvious and,on av-erage, accounts for 1-19%. In the case of nickel the tendency is similar,and the concentrations recorded in the upper researched soil layer are higher by 5.7-11.8%.

CONCLUSIONS

The experimental research findings show the increase in heavymetalconcentrationswhenthesoilisfertilizedwiththeliquidan-imalwaste.Copperconcentrationchangesfrom10.5to179.4 mg/kg at the soil depth of 10 cm and from 9.0 to 167.8 mg/kg at the soildepth of 10-20 cm.

One day after the waste application, copper concentrations exceed the permissible norms by 1.1-1.8 times,7 days after,these values become equal to the permissible ones,and 14days after they fall below the permissible ones.

Zinc concentration changes from 51.9 to 332.5 mg/kg at the soil depth of 0-10 cm and from 41.1 to 331.7 mg/kg at the soil depth of 10-20 cm. The set values at both depths were ex-ceeded only in the autumn season and only 1 day after the waste application by 1.1 times.The increase in concentrations of both copper and zinc are related to the nutrient additives that are used at the farm.Cr,Ni and Pb concentrations in the researched samples did not exceed the permissible quantities.

The concentrations of heavy metals depend on the time elapsed from the waste application onto the soil. After the so-lution is outpoured onto the soil, the concentrations rapidly increase and afterward start gradually decreasing. In 14 days copper concentrations decrease 2.9-8.5 times,those of chromi-um-1.2-1.3 times, lead -1.5-1.7 times, zinc -2.2-3.2 times, and nickel -1.5-1.9 times.

Depending on the time elapsed from the liquid animal waste application, in 14 days zinc concentration decreases in spring, on average, 2.2 times at the soil depth of 0-10 cm and around 2.6 times at the soil depth of 10-20 cm, in summer it falls by 2.8 and 3.2 times, in autumn 2.3 and 2.4 times, respectively. In 14 days from the waste application, in spring nickel concentration, on average, decreases by 1.7 times at the soil depth of 0-10 cm and 1.8 times at the soil depth of 10-20 cm,in summer -1.9 times, in autumn -1.5 times at both researched soil depths.

The concentrations of heavy metals depend on the soil sampling depth. The findings show that the concentration of zinc is by 2-3.6% lower at the second depth one day after the waste application.Afterseveraldays,theconcentrationsof heavy metals in the second depth are by 7-19% higher than in the first one.In the case of nickel this tendency remains similar,and the concentrations obtained in the upper researched layer are by 5.7-11.8% lower than those in the lower level.

OZONE DEPLETION

Ozone depletion describes two distinct, but related observations: a slow, steady decline of about 4 percent per decade in the total amount of ozone in Earth's stratosphere since the late 1970s; and a much larger, but seasonal, decrease in stratospheric ozone over Earth's polar regions during the same period. The latter phenomenon is commonly referred to as the ozone hole.

In addition to this well-known stratospheric ozone depletion, there are also tropospheric ozone depletion events, which occur near the surface in polar regions during spring.

The detailed mechanism by which the polar ozone holes form is different from that for the mid-latitude thinning, but the most important process in both trends is catalytic destruction of ozone by atomic chlorine and bromine. The main source of these halogen atoms in the stratosphere is photodissociation of chlorofluorocarbon (CFC) compounds, commonly called freons, and of bromofluorocarbon compounds known as halons. These compounds are transported into the stratosphere after being emitted at the surface. Both ozone depletion mechanisms strengthened as emissions of CFCs and halons increased.

CFCs and other contributory substances are commonly referred to as ozone-depleting substances (ODS). Since the ozone layer prevents most harmful UVB wavelengths (270-315 nm) of ultraviolet light (UV light) from passing through the Earth's atmosphere, observed and projected decreases in ozone have generated worldwide concern leading to adoption of the Montreal Protocol banning the production of CFCs and halons as well as related ozone depleting chemicals such as carbon tetrachloride and trichloroethane. It is suspected that a variety of biological consequences such as increases in skin cancer, damage to plants, and reduction of plankton populations in the ocean's photic zone may result from the increased UV exposure due to ozone depletion.

Ozone Cycle Overview

Three forms (or allotropes) of oxygen are involved in the ozone-oxygen cycle: Oxygen atoms (O or atomic oxygen), oxygen gas (O_2 or diatomic oxygen), and ozone gas (O_3 or triatomic oxygen). Ozone is formed in the stratosphere when oxygen molecules photodissociate after absorbing an ultraviolet photon whose wavelength is shorter than 240 nm. This produces two oxygen atoms. The atomic oxygen then combines with O_2 to create O_3. Ozone molecules absorb UV light between 310 and 200 nm, following which ozone splits into a molecule of O_2 and an oxygen atom. The oxygen atom then joins up with an oxygen molecule to regenerate ozone. This is a continuing process which terminates when an oxygen atom "recombines" with an ozone molecule to make two O_2 molecules:

$$O + O_3 \rightarrow 2O_2$$

The overall amount of ozone in the stratosphere is determined by a balance between photochemical production and recombination.

Ozone can be destroyed by a number of free radical catalysts, the most important of which are the hydroxyl radical (OH^-), the nitric oxide radical (NO^-) and atomic chlorine (Cl^-) and bromine (Br^-). All of these have both natural and anthropogenic (manmade) sources; at the present time, most of the OH^- and NO^- in the stratosphere is of natural origin, but human activity has dramatically increased the high in oxygen chlorine and bromine. These elements are found in certain stable organic compounds, especially chlorofluorocarbons (CFCs), which may find their way to the stratosphere without being destroyed in the troposphere due to their low reactivity. Once in the stratosphere, the Cl and Br atoms are liberated from the parent compounds by the action of ultraviolet light, e.g. ('h' is Planck's constant, 'ν' is frequency of electromagnetic radiation)

$$CFCl_3 + h\nu \rightarrow CFCl_2 + Cl$$

The Cl and Br atoms can then destroy ozone molecules through a variety of catalytic cycles. In the simplest example of such a cycle[2], a chlorine atom reacts with an ozone molecule, taking an oxygen atom with it (forming ClO) and leaving a normal oxygen molecule. A free oxygen atom then takes away the oxygen from the ClO, and the final result is an oxygen molecule and a chlorine atom, which then reinitiates the cycle. The chemical shorthand for these gas-phase reactions is:

$$Cl + O_3 \rightarrow ClO + O_2$$

$$ClO + O \rightarrow Cl + O_2$$

The net reaction is: $O_3 + O \rightarrow 2O_2$, the "recombination" reaction given above.

The overall effect is to increase the rate of recombination,leading to an overall decrease in the amount of ozone. For this particular mechanism to operate there must be a source of O atoms, which is primarily the photo dissociation of O3; thus this mechanism is only important in the upper stratosphere where such atoms are abundant. More complicated mechanisms have been discovered that lead to ozone destruction in the lower stratosphere as well.

A single chlorine atom would keep on destroying ozone for up to two years (the time scale for transport back down to the troposphere) were it not for reactions that remove them from this cycle by forming reservoir species such as hydrogen chloride (HCl) and chlorine nitrate ($ClONO_2$). On a per atom basis, bromine is even more efficient than chlorine at destroying ozone, but there is much less bromine in the atmosphere at present. As a result, both chlorine and bromine contribute significantly to the overall ozone depletion. Laboratory studies have shown that fluorine and iodine atoms participate in analogous catalytic cycles. However, in the Earth's stratosphere, fluorine atoms react rapidly with water and methane to form strongly-bound HF, while organic molecules which contain iodine react so rapidly in the lower atmosphere that they do not reach the stratosphere in significant quantities.

Observations

The most pronounced decrease in ozone has been in the lower stratosphere. However, the ozone hole is most usually measured not in terms of ozone concentrations at these levels (which are typically of a few parts per million) but by reduction in the total column ozone, above a point on the Earth's surface, which is normally expressed in Dobson units, abbreviated as "DU". Marked decreases in column ozone in the Antarctic spring and early summer compared to the early 1970s and before have been observed using instruments such as the Total Ozone Mapping Spectrometer (TOMS).

Reductions of up to 70% in the ozone column observed in the austral (southern hemispheric) spring over Antarctica and first reported in 1985 (Farman et al 1985) are continuing. Through the 1990s, total column ozone in September and October have continued to be 40-50% lower than pre-ozone-hole values. In the Arctic the amount lost is more variable year-to-year than in the Antarctic. The greatest declines, up to 30%, are in the winter and spring, when the stratosphere is colder.

Reactions that take place on polar stratospheric clouds (PSCs) play an important role in enhancing ozone depletion. PSCs form more readily in the extreme cold of Antarctic stratosphere. This is why ozone holes first formed, and are deeper, over Antarctica. Early models failed to take PSCs into account and predicted a gradual global depletion, which is why the sudden Antarctic ozone hole was such a surprise to many scientists.

In middle latitudes it is preferable to speak of ozone depletion rather than holes. Declines are about 3% below pre-1980 values for 35-60°N and about 6% for 35-60°S. In the tropics, there are no significant trends.

Ozone depletion also explains much of the observed reduction in stratospheric and upper tropospheric temperatures. The source of the warmth of the stratosphere is the absorption of UV radiation by ozone, hence reduced ozone leads to cooling. Some stratospheric cooling is also predicted from increases in greenhouse gases such as CO_2; however the ozone-induced cooling appears to be dominant.

Predictions of ozone levels remain difficult. The World Meteorological Organization Global Ozone Research and Monitoring Project-Report No. 44 comes out strongly in favor for the Montreal Protocol, but notes that a UNEP 1994 Assessment overestimated ozone loss for the 1994-1997 period.

Chemicals in the Atmosphere

CFCs in the Atmosphere

Chlorofluorocarbons (CFCs) were invented by Thomas Midgley in the 1920s. They were used in air conditioning/cooling units, as aerosol spray propellants prior to the 1980s, and in the cleaning processes of delicate electronic equipment. They also occur as by-products of some chemical processes. No significant natural sources have ever been identified for these compounds-their presence in the atmosphere is due almost entirely to human manufacture. As mentioned in the ozone cycle overview above, when such ozone-depleting chemicals reach the stratosphere, they are dissociated by ultraviolet light to release chlorine atoms. The chlorine atoms act as a catalyst, and each can break down tens of thousands of ozone molecules before being removed from the stratosphere. Given the longevity of CFC molecules, recovery times are measured in decades. It is calculated that a CFC molecule takes an average of 15 years to go from the ground level up to the upper atmosphere, and it can stay there for about a century, destroying up tc one hundred thousand ozone molecules during that time.

Verification of Observations

Scientists have been increasingly able to attribute the observed ozone depletion to the increase of anthropogenic halogen compounds from CFCs by the use of complex chemistry transport models and their validation against observational data (e.g. SLIMCAT, CLaMS). These models work by combining satellite measurements of chemical concentrations and meteorological fields with chemical reaction rate constants obtained in lab experiments. They are able to identify not only the key chemical reactions but also the transport processes which bring CFC photolysis products into contact with ozone.

The Ozone Hole and its Causes

The Antarctic ozone hole is an area of the Antarctic stratosphere in which the recent ozone levels have dropped to as low as 33% of their pre-1975 values. The ozone hole occurs during the Antarctic spring, from September to early December, as strong westerly winds start to circulate around the continent and create an atmospheric container. Within this "polar vortex", over 50% of the lower stratospheric ozone is destroyed during the Antarctic spring.

As explained above, the overall cause of ozone depletion is the presence of chlorine-containing source gases (primarily CFCs and related halocarbons). In the presence of UV light, these gases dissociate, releasing chlorine atoms, which then go on to catalyze ozone destruction. The Cl-catalyzed ozone depletion can take place in the gas phase, but it is dramatically enhanced in the presence of polar stratospheric clouds (PSCs).

These polar stratospheric clouds form during winter, in the extreme cold. Polar winters are dark, consisting of 3 months without solar radiation (sunlight). Not only lack of sunlight contributes to a decrease in temperature but also the "polar vortex" traps and chills air. Temperatures hover around or below -80 °C. These low temperatures form cloud particles and are composed of either nitric acid (Type I PSC) or ice (Type II PSC). Both types provide surfaces for chemical reactions that lead to ozone destruction.

The photochemical processes involved are complex but well understood. The key observation is that, ordinarily, most of the chlorine in the stratosphere resides in stable "reservoir" compounds, primarily hydrogen chloride (HCl) and chlorine nitrate ($ClONO_2$). During the Antarctic winter and spring, however, reactions on the surface of the polar stratospheric cloud particles convert these "reservoir" compounds into reactive free radicals (Cl and ClO). The clouds can also remove NO2 from the atmosphere by converting it to nitric acid, which prevents the newly formed ClO from being converted back into $ClONO_2$.

The role of sunlight in ozone depletion is the reason why the Antarctic ozone depletion is greatest during spring. During winter, even though PSCs are at their most abundant, there is no light over the pole to drive the chemical reactions. During the spring, however, the sun comes out, providing energy to drive photochemical reactions, and melt the polar stratospheric clouds, releasing the trapped compounds.

Most of the ozone that is destroyed is in the lower stratosphere, in contrast to the much smaller ozone depletion through homogeneous gas phase reactions, which occurs primarily in the upper stratosphere.

Warming temperatures near the end of spring break up the vortex around mid-December. As warm, ozone-rich air flows in from lower latitudes, the PSCs are destroyed, the ozone depletion process shuts down, and the ozone hole heals.

Interest in Ozone Depletion

While the effect of the Antarctic ozone hole in decreasing the global ozone is relatively small, estimated at about 4% per decade, the hole has generated a great deal of interest because:

- The decrease in the ozone layer was predicted in the early 1980s to be roughly 7% over a sixty-year period.
- The sudden recognition in 1985 that there was a substantial "hole" was widely reported in the press. The especially rapid ozone depletion in Antarctica had previously been dismissed as measurement error.

- Many were worried that ozone holes might start to appear over other areas of the globe but to date the only other large-scale depletion is a smaller ozone "dimple" observed during the Arctic spring over the North Pole. Ozone at middle latitudes has declined, but by a much smaller extent (about 4-5% decrease).
- If the conditions became more severe (cooler stratospheric temperatures, more stratospheric clouds, more active chlorine), then global ozone may decrease at a much greater pace. Standard global warming theory predicts that the stratosphere will cool.
- When the Antarctic ozone hole breaks up, the ozone-depleted air drifts out into nearby areas. Decreases in the ozone level of up to 10% have been reported in New Zealand in the month following the break-up of the Antarctic ozone hole

Consequences of Ozone Depletion

Since the ozone layer absorbs UVB ultraviolet light from the Sun, ozone layer depletion is expected to increase surface UVB levels, which could lead to damage, including increases in skin cancer. This was the reason for the Montreal Protocol. Although decreases in stratospheric ozone are well-tied to CFCs and there are good theoretical reasons to believe that decreases in ozone will lead to increases in surface UVB, there is no direct observational evidence linking ozone depletion to higher incidence of skin cancer in human beings. This is partly due to the fact that UVA, which has also been implicated in some forms of skin cancer, is not absorbed by ozone, and it is nearly impossible to control statistics for lifestyle changes in the populace.

Increased UV

Ozone, while a minority constituent in the earth's atmosphere, is responsible for most of the absorption of UVB radiation. The amount of UVB radiation that penetrates through the ozone layer decreases exponentially with the slant-path thickness/density of the layer. Correspondingly, a decrease in atmospheric ozone is expected to give rise to significantly increased levels of UVB near the surface.

Increases in surface UVB due to the ozone hole can be partially inferred by radiative transfer model calculations, but cannot be calculated from direct measurements because of the lack of reliable historical (pre-ozone-hole) surface UV data, although more recent surface UV observation measurement programmes exist (e.g. at Lauder, New Zealand).

Because it is this same UV radiation that creates ozone in the ozone layer from O_2 (regular oxygen) in the first place, a reduction in stratospheric ozone would actually tend to increase photochemical production of ozone at lower levels (in the troposphere), although the overall observed trends in total column ozone still show a decrease, largely because ozone produced lower down has a naturally shorter photochemical lifetime, so it is destroyed before the concentrations could reach a level which would compensate for the ozone reduction higher up.

Biological Effects of Increased UV

The main public concern regarding the ozone hole has been the effects of surface UV on human health. So far, ozone depletion in most locations has been typically a few percent. Were the high levels of depletion seen in the ozone hole ever to be common across the globe, the effects could be substantially more dramatic.

As the ozone hole over Antarctica has in some instances grown so large as to reach southern parts of Australia and New Zealand, environmentalists have been concerned that the increase in surface UV could be significant.

Effects on Humans

UVB (the higher energy UV radiation absorbed by ozone) is generally accepted to be a contributory factor to skin cancer. In addition, increased surface UV leads to increased tropospheric ozone, which is a health risk to humans. The increased surface UV also represents an increase in the vitamin D synthetic capacity of the sunlight. The cancer preventive effects of vitamin D represent a possible beneficial effect of ozone depletion. In terms of health costs, the possible benefits of increased UV irradiance may outweigh the burden.

Basal and Squamous Cell Carcinomas: The most common forms of skin cancer in humans, basal and squamous cell carcinomas, have been strongly linked to UVB exposure. The mechanism by which UVB induces these cancers is well understood-absorption of UVB radiation causes the pyrimidine bases in the DNA molecule to form dimers, resulting in transcription errors when the DNA replicates.

These cancers are relatively mild and rarely fatal, although the treatment of squamous cell carcinoma sometimes requires extensive reconstructive surgery. By combining epidemiological data with results of animal studies, scientists have estimated that a one percent decrease in stratospheric ozone would increase the incidence of these cancers by 2%.

Malignant Melanoma: Another form of skin cancer, malignant melanoma, is much less common but far more dangerous, being lethal in about 15% -20% of the cases diagnosed. The relationship between malignant melanoma and ultraviolet exposure is not yet well understood, but it appears that both UVB and UVA are involved.

Experiments on fish suggest that 90 to 95% of malignant melanomas may be due to UVA and visible radiation whereas experiments on opossums suggest a larger role for UVB. Because of this uncertainty, it is difficult to estimate the impact of ozone depletion on melanoma incidence. One study showed that a 10% increase in UVB radiation was associated with a 19% increase in melanomas for men and 16% for women. A study of people in Punta Arenas, at the southern tip of Chile, showed a 56% increase in melanoma and a 46% increase in nonmelanoma skin cancer over a period of seven years, along with decreased ozone and increased UVB levels.

Cortical Cataracts: Studies are suggestive of an association between ocular cortical cataracts and UV-B exposure, using crude approximations of exposure and various cataract assessment techniques. A detailed assessment of ocular exposure to UV-B was carried out in a study on Chesapeake Bay Watermen, where increases in average annual ocular exposure were associated with increasing risk of cortical opacity.

In this highly exposed group of predominantly white males, the evidence linking cortical opacities to sunlight exposure was the strongest to date. However, subsequent data from a population-based study in Beaver Dam, WI suggested the risk may be confined to men.

In the Beaver Dam study, the exposures among women were lower than exposures among men, and no association was seen. Moreover, there were no data linking sunlight exposure to risk of cataract in African Americans, although other eye diseases have different prevalences among the different racial groups, and cortical opacity appears to be higher in African Americans compared with whites.

Increased Tropospheric Ozone: Increased surface UV leads to increased tropospheric ozone. Ground-level ozone is generally recognized to be a health risk, as ozone is toxic due to its strong oxidant properties. At this time, ozone at ground level is produced mainly by the action of UV radiation on combustion gases from vehicle exhausts.

Effects on Crops

An increase of UV radiation would be expected to affect crops. A number of economically important species of plants, such as rice, depend on cyanobacteria residing on their roots for the retention of nitrogen. Cyanobacteria are sensitive to UV light and they would be affected by its increase.

Effects on Plankton

Research has shown a widespread extinction of plankton 2 million years ago that coincided with a nearby supernova. There is a difference in the orientation and motility of planktons when excess of UV rays reach earth. Researchers speculate that the extinction was caused by a significant weakening of the ozone layer at that time when the radiation from the supernova produced nitrogen oxides that catalyzed the destruction of ozone (plankton are particularly susceptible to effects of UV light, and are vitally important to marine food webs).

Public Policy in Response to the Ozone Hole

The full extent of the damage that CFCs have caused to the ozone layer is not known and will not be known for decades; however, marked decreases in column ozone have already been observed.

After a 1976 report by the U.S. National Academy of Sciences concluded that credible scientific evidence supported the ozone depletion hypothesis, a few countries, including the United States, Canada, Sweden, and Norway, moved to eliminate the use of CFCs in aerosol spray cans. At the time this was widely regarded as a first step towards a more comprehensive regulation policy, but progress in this direction slowed in subsequent years, due to a combination of political factors (continued resistance from the halocarbon industry and a general change in attitude towards environmental regulation during the first two years of the Reagan administration) and scientific developments (subsequent National Academy assessments which indicated that the first estimates of the magnitude of ozone depletion had been overly large). The European Community rejected proposals to ban CFCs in aerosol sprays while even in the U.S., CFCs continued to be used as refrigerants and for cleaning circuit boards. Worldwide CFC production fell sharply after the U.S. aerosol ban, but by 1986 had returned nearly to its 1976 level. In 1980, DuPont closed down its research program into halocarbon alternatives.

The US Government's attitude began to change again in 1983, when William Ruckelshaus replaced Anne M. Burford as Administrator of the United States Environmental Protection Agency. Under Ruckelshaus and his successor, Lee Thomas, the EPA pushed for an international approach to halocarbon regulations. In 1985 20 nations, including most of the major CFC producers, signed the Vienna Convention which established a framework for negotiating international regulations on ozone-depleting substances. That same year, the discovery of the Antarctic ozone hole was announced, causing a revival in public attention to the issue. In 1987, representatives from 43 nations signed the Montreal Protocol. Meanwhile, the halocarbon industry shifted its position and started supporting a protocol to limit CFC production. The reasons for this were in part explained by "Dr. Mostafa Tolba, former head of the UN Environment Programme, who was quoted in the June 30, 1990 edition of The New Scientist, '...the chemical industry supported the Montreal Protocol in 1987 because it set up a worldwide schedule for phasing out CFCs, which [were] no longer protected by patents. This provided companies with an equal opportunity to market new, more profitable compounds.'"

At Montreal, the participants agreed to freeze production of CFCs at 1986 levels and to reduce production by 50% by

1999. After a series of scientific expeditions to the Antarctic produced convincing evidence that the ozone hole was indeed caused by chlorine and bromine from manmade organohalogens, the Montreal Protocol was strengthened at a 1990 meeting in London. The participants agreed to phase out CFCs and halons entirely (aside from a very small amount marked for certain "essential" uses, such as asthma inhalers) by 2000. At a 1992 meeting in Copenhagen, the phase out date was moved up to 1996.

To some extent, CFCs have been replaced by the less damaging hydro-chloro-fluoro-carbons (HCFCs), although concerns remain regarding HCFCs also. In some applications, hydro-fluoro-carbons (HFCs) have been used to replace CFCs. HFCs, which contain no chlorine or bromine, do not contribute at all to ozone depletion although they are potent greenhouse gases. The best known of these compounds is probably HFC-134a (R-134a), which in the United States has largely replaced CFC-12 (R-12) in automobile air conditioners.

Ozone Diplomacy, by Richard Benedick (Harvard University Press, 1991) gives a detailed account of the negotiation process that led to the Montreal Protocol. Pielke and Betsill provide an extensive review of early US government responses to the emerging science of ozone depletion by CFCs.

Current Events and Future Prospects of Ozone Depletion

Since the adoption and strengthening of the Montreal Protocol has led to reductions in the emissions of CFCs, atmospheric concentrations of the most significant compounds have been declining. These substances are being gradually removed from the atmosphere. By 2015, the Antarctic ozone hole would have reduced by only 1 million km^2 out of 25 (Newman et al., 2004); complete recovery of the Antarctic ozone layer will not occur until the year 2050 or later. Work has suggested that a detectable (and statistically significant) recovery will not occur until around 2024, with ozone levels recovering to 1980 levels by around 2068.

There is a slight caveat to this, however. Global warming from CO_2 is expected to cool the stratosphere. This, in turn, would lead to a relative increase in ozone depletion and the frequency of ozone holes. The effect may not be linear; ozone holes form because of polar stratospheric clouds; the formation of polar stratospheric clouds has a temperature threshold above which they will not form; cooling of the Arctic stratosphere might lead to Antarctic-ozone-hole-like conditions. But at the moment this is not clear.

Even though the stratosphere as a whole is cooling, high-latitude areas may become increasingly predisposed to springtime stratospheric warming events as weather patterns change in response to higher greenhouse gas loading. This would cause PSCs to disappear earlier in the season, and may explain why Antarctic ozone hole seasons have tended to end somewhat earlier since 2000 as compared with the most prolonged ozone holes of the 1990s.

The decrease in ozone-depleting chemicals has also been significantly affected by a decrease in bromine-containing chemicals. The data suggest that substantial natural sources exist for atmospheric methyl bromide (CH3Br).

The 2004 ozone hole ended in November 2004, daily minimum stratospheric temperatures in the Antarctic lower stratosphere increased to levels that are too warm for the formation of polar stratospheric clouds (PSCs) about 2 to 3 weeks earlier than in most recent years.

The Arctic winter of 2005 was extremely cold in the stratosphere; PSCs were abundant over many high-latitude areas until dissipated by a big warming event, which started in the upper stratosphere during February and spread throughout the Arctic stratosphere in March. The size of the

Arctic area of anomalously low total ozone in 2004-2005 was larger than in any year since 1997. The predominance of anomalously low total ozone values in the Arctic region in the winter of 2004-2005 is attributed to the very low stratospheric temperatures and meteorological conditions favorable for ozone destruction along with the continued presence of ozone destroying chemicals in the stratosphere.

A 2005 IPCC summary of ozone issues observed that observations and model calculations suggest that the global average amount of ozone depletion has now approximately stabilized. Although considerable variability in ozone is expected from year to year, including in polar regions where depletion is largest, the ozone layer is expected to begin to recover in coming decades due to declining ozone-depleting substance concentrations, assuming full compliance with the Montreal Protocol.

Temperatures during the Arctic winter of 2006 stayed fairly close to the long-term average until late January, with minimum readings frequently cold enough to produce PSCs. During the last week of January, however, a major warming event sent temperatures well above normal-much too warm to support PSCs. By the time temperatures dropped back to near normal in March, the seasonal norm was well above the PSC threshold. Preliminary satellite instrument-generated ozone maps show seasonal ozone buildup slightly below the long-term means for the Northern Hemisphere as a whole, although some high ozone events have occurred. During March 2006, the Arctic stratosphere poleward of 60 degrees North Latitude was free of anomalously low ozone areas except during the three-day period from March 17 to 19 when the total ozone cover fell below 300 DU over part of the North Atlantic region from Greenland to Scandinavia.

The area where total column ozone is less than 220 DU (the accepted definition of the boundary of the ozone hole) was relatively small until around 20 August 2006. Since then the ozone hole area increased rapidly, peaking at 29 million km^2 September 24. In October 2006, NASA reported that the year's ozone hole set a new area record with a daily average of 26 million km^2 between 7 September and 13 October 2006; total ozone thicknesses fell as low as 85 DU on October 8. The two factors combined, 2006 sees the worst level of depletion in recorded ozone history. The depletion is attributed to the temperatures above the Antarctic reaching the lowest recording since comprehensive records began in 1979.

The Antarctic ozone hole is expected to continue for decades. Ozone concentrations in the lower stratosphere over Antarctica will increase by 5%-10% by 2020 and return to pre-1980 levels by about 2060-2075, 10-25 years later than predicted in earlier assessments. This is because of revised estimates of atmospheric concentrations of Ozone Depleting Substances-and a larger predicted future usage in developing countries. Another factor which may aggravate ozone depletion is the draw-down of nitrogen oxides from above the stratosphere due to changing wind patterns.

History of the Research

The basic physical and chemical processes that lead to the formation of an ozone layer in the earth's stratosphere were discovered by Sydney Chapman in 1930. These are discussed in the article Ozone-oxygen cycle-briefly, short-wavelength UV radiation splits an oxygen (O_2) molecule into two oxygen (O) atoms, which then combine with other oxygen molecules to form ozone. Ozone is removed when an oxygen atom and an ozone molecule "recombine" to form two oxygen molecules, i.e. $O + O_3 \rightarrow 2O_2$. In the 1950s, David Bates and Marcel Nicolet presented evidence that various free radicals, in particular hydroxyl (OH) and nitric oxide (NO), could catalyze this recombination reaction, reducing the overall amount of ozone. These free radicals were known to be present in the stratosphere, and so were regarded as part of the natural balance-it was estimated that in their absence, the ozone layer would be about twice as thick as it currently is.

In 1970 Prof. Paul Crutzen pointed out that emissions of nitrous oxide (N_2O), a stable, long-lived gas produced by soil bacteria, from the earth's surface could affect the amount of nitric oxide (NO) in the stratosphere. Crutzen showed that nitrous oxide lives long enough to reach the stratosphere, where it is converted into NO. Crutzen then noted that increasing use of fertilizers might have led to an increase in nitrous oxide emissions over the natural background, which would in turn result in an increase in the amount of NO in the stratosphere. Thus human activity could have an impact on the stratospheric ozone layer. In the following year, Crutzen and (independently) Harold Johnston suggested that NO emissions from supersonic aircraft, which fly in the lower stratosphere, could also deplete the ozone layer.

The Rowland-Molina Hypothesis

In 1974 Frank Sherwood Rowland, a Chemistry Professor at the University of California at Irvine, and his postdoctoral associate Mario J. Molina suggested that long-lived organic halogen compounds, such as CFCs, might behave in a similar fashion as Crutzen had proposed for nitrous oxide. James Lovelock (most popularly known as the creator of the Gaia hypothesis) had recently discovered, during a cruise in the South Atlantic in 1971, that almost all of the CFC compounds manufactured since their invention in 1930 were still present in the atmosphere. Molina and Rowland concluded that, like N_2O, the CFCs would reach the stratosphere where they would be dissociated by UV light, releasing Cl atoms. (A year earlier, Richard Stolarski and Ralph Cicerone at the University of Michigan had shown that Cl is even more efficient than NO at catalyzing the destruction of ozone. Similar conclusions were reached by Michael McElroy and Steven Wofsy at Harvard University. Neither group, however, had realized that CFC's were a potentially large source of stratospheric chlorine-instead, they had been investigating the possible effects of HCl emissions from the Space Shuttle, which are very much smaller.)

The Rowland-Molina hypothesis was strongly disputed by representatives of the aerosol and halocarbon industries. The Chair of the Board of DuPont was quoted as saying that ozone depletion theory is "a science fiction tale...a load of rubbish...utter nonsense".

Robert Abplanalp, the President of Precision Valve Corporation (and inventor of the first practical aerosol spray can valve), wrote to the Chancellor of UC Irvine to complain about Rowland's public statements (Roan, p 56.) Nevertheless, within three years most of the basic assumptions made by Rowland and Molina were confirmed by laboratory measurements and by direct observation in the stratosphere. The concentrations of the source gases (CFC's and related compounds) and the chlorine reservoir species (HCl and $ClONO_2$) were measured throughout the stratosphere, and demonstrated that CFCs were indeed the major source of stratospheric chlorine, and that nearly all of the CFCs emitted would eventually reach the stratosphere. Even more convincing was the measurement, by James G. Anderson and collaborators, of chlorine monoxide (ClO) in the stratosphere. ClO is produced by the reaction of Cl with ozone-its observation thus demonstrated that Cl radicals not only were present in the stratosphere but also were actually involved in destroying ozone.

McElroy and Wofsy extended the work of Rowland and Molina by showing that Bromine atoms were even more effective catalysts for ozone loss than chlorine atoms and argued that the brominated organic compounds known as halons, widely used in fire extinguishers, were a potentially large source of stratospheric bromine. In 1976 the U.S. National Academy of Sciences released a report which concluded that the ozone depletion hypothesis was strongly supported by the scientific evidence. Scientists calculated that if CFC production continued to increase at the going rate of 10% per year until 1990 and then remain steady, CFCs would cause a global ozone loss of 5 to 7% by 1995, and a 30 to 50% loss by 2050. In response the United States, Canada, Sweden and Norway banned the use of CFCs in aerosol spray cans in 1978. However, subsequent research, summarized by the National Academy in reports issued between 1979 and 1984, appeared to show that the earlier estimates of global ozone loss had been too large.

The Ozone Hole

The discovery of the Antarctic "ozone hole" by British Antarctic Survey scientists Farman, Gardiner and Shanklin (announced in a paper in Nature in May 1985) came as a shock to the scientific community, because the observed decline in polar ozone was far larger than anyone had anticipated. Satellite measurements showing massive depletion of ozone around the south pole were becoming available at the same time. However, these were initially rejected as unreasonable by data quality control algorithms (they were filtered out as errors since the values were unexpectedly low); the ozone hole was detected only in satellite data when the raw data was reprocessed following evidence of ozone depletion in in situ observations. When the software was rerun without the flags, the ozone hole was seen as far back as 1976.

Susan Solomon, an atmospheric chemist at the National Oceanic and Atmospheric Administration (NOAA), proposed that chemical reactions on polar stratospheric clouds (PSCs) in the cold Antarctic stratosphere caused a massive, though localized and seasonal, increase in the amount of chlorine present in active, ozone-destroying forms. The polar stratospheric clouds in Antarctica are only formed when there are very low temperatures, as low as-80 degrees C, and early spring conditions. In such conditions the ice crystals of the cloud provide a suitable surface for conversion of unreactive chlorine compounds into reactive chlorine compounds which can deplete ozone easily.

Moreover the polar vortex formed over Antarctica is very tight and the reaction which occurs on the surface of the cloud crystals is far different from when it occurs in atmosphere. These conditions have led to ozone hole formation in Antarctica. This hypothesis was decisively confirmed, first by laboratory measurements and subsequently by direct measurements, from the ground and from high-altitude airplanes, of very high concentrations of chlorine monoxide (ClO) in the Antarctic stratosphere. Alternative hypotheses, which had attributed the ozone hole to variations in solar UV radiation or to changes in atmospheric circulation patterns, were also tested and shown to be untenable.

Meanwhile, analysis of ozone measurements from the worldwide network of ground-based Dobson spectrophoto-meters led an international panel to conclude that the ozone layer was in fact being depleted, at all latitudes outside of the tropics. These trends were confirmed by satellite measurements. As a consequence, the major halocarbon producing nations agreed to phase out production of CFCs, halons, and related compounds, a process that was completed in 1996. Crutzen, Molina, and Rowland were awarded the 1995 Nobel Prize in Chemistry for their work on stratospheric ozone.

Since 1981 the United Nations Environment Programme has sponsored a series of reports on scientific assessment of ozone depletion. The most recent is from 2007 where satellite measurements have shown the hole in the ozone layer is recovering and is now the smallest it has been for about a decade.

Controversy Regarding Ozone Science and Policy

That ozone depletion takes place is not seriously disputed in the scientific community. There is a consensus among atmospheric physicists and chemists that the scientific understanding has now reached a level where countermeasures to control CFC emissions are justified, although the decision is ultimately one for policy-makers.

Despite this consensus, the science behind ozone depletion remains complex, and some who oppose the enforcement of countermeasures point to some of the uncertainties. For example, although increased UVB has been shown to constitute a melanoma risk, it has been difficult for statistical studies to establish a direct link between ozone depletion and increased rates of melanoma. Although melanomas did increase significantly during the period 1970-1990, it is difficult to separate reliably the effect of ozone depletion from the effect of changes in lifestyle factors (e.g., increasing rates of air travel).

Ozone Depletion and Global Warming

Although they are often interlinked in the mass media, the connection between global warming and ozone depletion is not strong. There are four areas of linkage:

- The same CO_2 radiative forcing that produces near-surface global warming is expected to cool the stratosphere. This cooling, in turn, is expected to produce a relative increase in ozone (O_3) depletion and the frequency of ozone holes.
- Conversely, ozone depletion represents a radiative forcing of the climate system. There are two opposing

effects: Reduced ozone causes the stratosphere to absorb less solar radiation, thus cooling the stratosphere while warming the troposphere; the resulting colder stratosphere emits less long-wave radiation downward, thus cooling the troposphere. Overall, the cooling dominates; the IPCC concludes that "observed stratospheric O_3 losses over the past two decades have caused a negative forcing of the surface-troposphere system" of about -0.15 ± 0.10 watts per square meter (W/m^2).

- One of the strongest predictions of the greenhouse effect theory is that the stratosphere will cool. Although this cooling has been observed, it is not trivial to separate the effects of changes in the concentration of greenhouse gases and ozone depletion since both will lead to cooling. However, this can be done by numerical stratospheric modeling. Results from the National Oceanic and Atmospheric Administration's Geophysical Fluid Dynamics Laboratory show that above 20 km (12.4 miles), the greenhouse gases dominate the cooling.
- Ozone depleting chemicals are also greenhouse gases. The increases in concentrations of these chemicals have produced 0.34 ± 0.03 W/m^2 of radiative forcing, corresponding to about 14% of the total radiative forcing from increases in the concentrations of well-mixed greenhouse gases.

Misconceptions about Ozone Depletion

A few of the more common misunderstandings about ozone depletion are addressed briefly here; more detailed discussions can be found in the ozone-depletion FAQ.

CFCs are "Too Heavy" to Reach the Stratosphere

It is sometimes stated that since CFC molecules are much heavier than nitrogen or oxygen, they cannot reach the stratosphere in significant quantities. But atmospheric gases are not sorted by weight; the forces of wind (turbulence) are strong enough to fully intermix gases in the atmosphere. CFCs are heavier than air, but just like argon, krypton and other heavy gases with a long lifetime, they are uniformly distributed throughout the turbosphere and reach the upper atmosphere.

Man-made Chlorine is Insignificant Compared to Natural Sources

Another objection occasionally voiced is that It is generally agreed that natural sources of tropospheric chlorine (volcanoes, ocean spray, etc.) are four to five orders of magnitude larger than man-made sources. While strictly true, tropospheric chlorine is irrelevant; it is stratospheric chlorine that matters to ozone depletion. Chlorine from ocean spray is soluble and thus is washed out by rainfall before it reaches the stratosphere.

CFCs, in contrast, are insoluble and long-lived, which allows them to reach the stratosphere. Even in the lower atmosphere there is more chlorine present in the form of CFCs and related haloalkanes than there is in HCl from salt spray, and in the stratosphere the halocarbons dominate overwhelmingly. Only one of these halocarbons, methyl chloride, has a predominantly natural source, and it is responsible for about 20 percent of the chlorine in the stratosphere; the remaining 80% comes from manmade compounds.

Very large volcanic eruptions can inject HCl directly into the stratosphere, but direct measurements have shown that their contribution is small compared to that of chlorine from CFCs. A similar erroneous assertion is that soluble halogen compounds from the volcanic plume of Mount Erebus on Ross Island, Antarctica are a major contributor to the Antarctic ozone hole.

An Ozone Hole was First Observed in 1956

G.M.B. Dobson (Exploring the Atmosphere, 2nd Edition, Oxford, 1968) mentioned that when springtime ozone levels over Halley Bay were first measured, he was surprised to find that they were ~320 DU, about 150 DU below spring levels, ~450 DU, in the Arctic. These, however, were the pre-ozone hole normal climatological values. What Dobson describes is essentially the baseline from which the ozone hole is measured: actual ozone hole values are in the 150-100 DU range.

The discrepancy between the Arctic and Antarctic noted by Dobson was primarily a matter of timing: during the Arctic spring ozone levels rose smoothly, peaking in April, whereas in the Antarctic they stayed approximately constant during early spring, rising abruptly in November when the polar vortex broke down.

The behavior seen in the Antarctic ozone hole is completely different. Instead of staying constant, early springtime ozone levels suddenly drop from their already low winter values, by as much as 50%, and normal values are not reached again until December.

If the Theory were Correct, the Ozone Hole should be Above the Sources of CFCs

CFCs are well mixed in the troposphere and the stratosphere. The reason the ozone hole occurs above Antarctica is not because there are more CFCs there but because the low temperatures allow polar stratospheric clouds to form. There have been anomalous discoveries of significant, serious, localized "holes" above other parts of the globe.

The "Ozone Hole" is a Hole in the Ozone Layer

When the "ozone hole" forms, essentially all of the ozone in the lower stratosphere is destroyed. The upper stratosphere is much less affected, however, so that the overall amount of ozone over the continent declines by 50 percent or more. The ozone hole does not go all the way through the layer; on the other hand, it is not a uniform 'thinning' of the layer either. It's a "hole" in the sense of "a hole in the ground", a depression, not in the sense of "a hole in the windshield."

ACID RAIN

Acid rain is rain or any other form of precipitation which is unusually acidic. It has harmful effects on plants, aquatic animals and buildings. Acid rain is mostly caused by human emissions of sulfur and nitrogen compounds which react in the atmosphere to produce acids. In recent years, many governments have introduced laws to reduce these emissions.

Definition

The term "acid rain" is commonly used to mean the deposition of acidic components in rain, snow, fog, dew, or dry particles. The more accurate term is "acid precipitation." Distilled water, which contains no carbon dioxide, has a neutral pH of 7. Liquids with a pH less than 7 are acidic, and those with a pH greater than 7 are bases. "Clean" or unpolluted rain is slightly acidic, its pH being about 5.0, because carbon dioxide and water in the air react together to form carbonic acid, a weak acid.

$$H_2O\ (l) + CO_2\ (g) \rightarrow H_2CO_3\ (aq)$$

Carbonic acid then can ionize in water forming low concentrations of hydronium ions:

$$2H_2O\ (l) + H_2CO_3\ (aq) \rightarrow CO_3^{2-}(aq) + 2H_3O^+(aq)$$

The extra acidity in rain comes from the reaction of primary air pollutants, primarily sulfur oxides and nitrogen oxides, with water in the air to form strong acids (like sulfuric and nitric acid). The main sources of these pollutants are vehicles and industrial and power-generating plants.

History

Since the Industrial Revolution, emissions of sulfur dioxide and nitrogen oxides to the atmosphere have increased. Acid rain was first found in Manchester, England. In 1852, Robert Angus Smith found the relationship between acid rain and atmospheric pollution. Though acid rain was discovered in 1852, it wasn't until the late 1960s that scientists began widely observing and studying the phenomenon. Canadian Harold Harvey was among the first to research a "dead" lake. Public awareness of acid rain in the U.S increased in the 1990s after the New York Times promulgated reports from the Hubbard Brook Experimental Forest in New Hampshire of the myriad deleterious environmental effects demonstrated to result from it.

Occasional pH readings of well below 2.4 (the acidity of vinegar) have been reported in industrialized areas. Industrial acid rain is a substantial problem in China, Eastern Europe, Russia and areas down-wind from them. These areas all burn sulfur-containing coal to generate heat and electricity. The problem of acid rain not only has increased with population and industrial growth, but has become more widespread.

The use of tall smokestacks to reduce local pollution has contributed to the spread of acid rain by releasing gases into regional atmospheric circulation. Often deposition occurs a considerable distance downwind of the emissions, with mountainous regions tending to receive the most (simply because of their higher rainfall). An example of this effect is the low pH of rain (compared to the local emissions) which falls in Scandinavia.

Emissions of Chemicals Leading to Acidification

The most important gas which leads to acidification is sulfur dioxide. Emissions of nitrogen oxides which are oxidized to form nitric acid are of increasing importance due to stricter controls on emissions of sulfur containing compounds. 70 Tg(S) per year in the form of SO_2 comes from fossil fuel combustion and industry, 2.8 Tg(S) from wildfires and 7-8 Tg(S) per year from volcanoes.

Natural Phenomena

The principal natural phenomena that contribute acid-producing gases to the atmosphere are emissions from volcanoes and those from biological processes that occur on the land, in wetlands, and in the oceans. The major biological source of sulfur containing compounds is dimethyl sulfide.

The effects of acidic deposits have been detected in glacial ice thousands of years old in remote parts of the globe.

Human Activity

The principal cause of acid rain is sulfur-and nitrogen compounds from human sources, such as electricity generation, factories and motor vehicles. Coal power plants are one of the most polluting. The gases can be carried hundreds of kilometres in the atmosphere before they are converted to acids and deposited. In the past, factories had short funnels to let out smoke, but this caused many problems; thus, factories now have longer smoke funnels. However, this causes pollutants to be carried farther, causing greater ecological damage.

Chemical Processes

Gas Phase Chemistry

In the gas phase sulfur dioxide is oxidized by reaction with the hydroxyl radical via a intermolecular reaction:

$$SO_2 + OH^- \rightarrow HOSO_2\cdot$$

which is followed by:

$$HOSO_2\cdot + O_2 \rightarrow HO_2\cdot + SO_3$$

In the presence of water sulfur trioxide (SO_3) is converted rapidly to sulfuric acid:

$$SO_3(g) + H_2O(l) \rightarrow H_2SO_4(l)$$

Nitric acid is formed by the reaction of OH with Nitrogen dioxide:

$$NO_2 + OH\cdot \rightarrow HNO_3$$

For more information see Seinfeld and Pandis (1998).[2]

Chemistry in cloud droplets

When clouds are present the loss rate of SO_2 is faster than can be explained by gas phase chemistry alone. This is due to reactions in the liquid water droplets

Hydrolysis

Sulfur dioxide dissolves in water and then, like carbon dioxide, hydrolyses in a series of equilibrium reactions:

$$SO_2\,(g) + H_2O \rightarrow SO_2\cdot H_2O$$

$$SO_2\cdot H_2O \rightarrow H^+ + HSO_3^-$$

$$HSO_3^- \rightarrow H^+ + SO_3^{2-}$$

Oxidation

There are a large number of aqueous reactions that oxidize sulfur from S(IV) to S(VI), leading to the formation of sulfuric acid. The most important oxidation reactions are with ozone, hydrogen peroxide and oxygen (reactions with oxygen are catalyzed by iron and manganese in the cloud droplets).

Acid Deposition

Wet Deposition

Wet deposition of acids occurs when any form of precipitation (rain, snow, etc) removes acids from the atmosphere and delivers it to the Earth's surface. This can result from the deposition of acids produced in the raindrops (see aqueous phase chemistry above) or by the precipitation removing the acids either in clouds or below clouds. Wet removal of both gases and aerosol are both of importance for wet deposition.

Dry Deposition

Acid deposition also occurs via dry deposition in the absence of precipitation. This can be responsible for as much as 20 to 60% of total acid deposition. This occurs when particles and gases stick to the ground, plants or other surfaces.

Adverse Effects

Acid rain has been shown to have adverse impacts on forests, freshwaters and soils, killing off insect and aquatic lifeforms as well as causing damage to buildings and having possible impacts on human health.

Surface Waters and Aquatic Animals

Both the lower pH and higher aluminum concentrations in surface water that occur as a result of acid rain can cause damage to fish and other aquatic animals. At pHs lower than 5 most fish eggs will not hatch and lower pHs can kill adult fish. As lakes become more acidic biodiversity is reduced. Acid rain has eliminated insect life and some fish species, including the brook trout in some Appalachian streams and creeks.

However, there has been some debate on the extent to which acid rain contributes to lake acidity (i.e., that many acid lakes may result primarily from characteristics of the surrounding watershed, and not the rain itself). The EPA's website states: "Of the lakes and streams surveyed, acid rain caused acidity in 75 percent of the acidic lakes and about 50 percent of the acidic streams".

Soils

Soil biology can be seriously damaged by acid rain. Some tropical microbes can quickly consume acids[11] but other microbes are unable to tolerate low pHs and are killed. The enzymes of these microbes are denatured (changed in shape so they no longer function) by the acid. The hydronium ions of acid rain also mobilize toxins and leach away essential nutrients and minerals.

$$nH^{+}\ (aq)^{+}\ Mn^{2+}\ (clay) \rightarrow nH^{+}\ (clay)^{+}\ Mn_2^{+}(aq)$$

Forests and other Vegetation

Acid rain can slow the growth of vulnerable forests and cause leaves and needles to turn brown and fall off. Adverse effects may be indirectly related to acid rain, like the acid's effects on soil or high concentration of gaseous precursors to acid rain. High altitude forests are especially vulnerable as they are often surrounded by clouds and fog which are more acidic than rain.

Other plants can also be damaged by acid rain but the effect on food crops is minimized by the application of fertilizers to replace lost nutrients. In cultivated areas, limestone may also be added to increase the ability of the soil to keep the pH stable, but this tactic is largely unusable in the case of wilderness lands. Acid Rain depletes minerals from the soil and then it stunts the growth of the plant.

Human Health

Some scientists have suggested direct links to human health, but none have been proven. However, fine particles, a large fraction of which are formed from the same gases as acid rain (sulphur dioxide and nitrogen dioxide), have been shown to cause illness and premature deaths such as cancer and other deadly diseases.

Other Adverse Effects

Acid rain can also cause damage to certain building materials and historical monuments. This is because the sulfuric acid in the rain chemically reacts with the calcium compounds in the stones (limestone, sandstone, marble and granite) to create gypsum, which then flakes off.

$$CaCO_3 \text{ (s)} + H_2SO_4 \text{ (aq)} \rightarrow CaSO_4 \text{ (aq)} + CO_2 \text{ (g)} + H_2O \text{ (l)}$$

This is also commonly seen on old gravestones where the acid rain can cause the inscription to become completely illegible. Acid rain also causes an increased rate of oxidation for iron. Visibility is also reduced by sulfate and nitrate in the atmosphere.

Prevention Methods

Technical Solutions

In the United States, many coal-burning power plants use Flue gas desulfurization (FGD) to remove sulphur-containing gases from their stack gases. An example of FGD is the wet scrubber which is commonly used in the U.S. and many other countries. A wet scrubber is basically a reaction tower equipped with a fan that extracts hot smoke stack gases from a power plant into the tower.

Lime or limestone in slurry form is also injected into the tower to mix with the stack gases and combine with the sulphur dioxide present. The calcium carbonate of the limestone produces pH-neutral calcium sulfate that is physically removed from the scrubber. That is, the scrubber turns sulfur pollution into industrial sulfates.

In some areas the sulfates are sold to chemical companies as gypsum when the purity of calcium sulfate is high. In others, they are placed in landfill. However, the effects of acid rain can last for generations, as the effects of pH level change can stimulate the continued leaching of undesirable chemicals into otherwise pristine water sources, killing off vulnerable insect and fish species and blocking efforts to restore native life.

Automobile emissions control reduces emissions of nitrogen oxides from motor vehicles.

International Treaties

A number of international treaties on the long range transport of atmospheric pollutants have been agreed e.g. Sulphur Emissions Reduction Protocol under the Convention on Long-Range Transboundary Air Pollution.

Emissions Trading

A more recent regulatory scheme involves emissions trading. In this scheme, every current polluting facility is given an emissions license that becomes part of capital equipment. Operators can then install pollution control equipment, and sell parts of their emissions licenses. The intention of this is to give operators economic incentives to install pollution controls.

HEALTH EFFECTS OF AIR POLLUTION

The human health effects of poor air quality are far reaching, but principally affect the body's respiratory system and the cardiovascular system. Individual reactions to air pollutants depend on the type of pollutant a person is exposed to, the degree of exposure, the individual's health status and genetics. People who exercise outdoors, for example, on hot, smoggy days increase their exposure to pollutants in the air.

The health effects caused by air pollutants may range from subtle biochemical and physiological changes to difficulty breathing, wheezing, coughing and aggravation of existing respiratory and cardiac conditions. These effects can result in increased medication use, increased doctor or emergency room visits, more hospital admissions and even premature death.

- Human Respiratory System
- Human Cardiovascular System
- Heart and Lung Diseases
- Pyramid of Health Effects
- Populations at Risk
- Leading Causes of Hospitalization
- Leading Causes of Death
- Estimating Health Benefits

Human Respiratory System

The health of our lungs and entire respiratory system is affected by the quality of the air we breathe. In addition to oxygen, this air contains other substances such as pollutants, which can be harmful. Exposure to chemicals by inhalation can negatively affect our lungs and other organs in the body.

The respiratory system is particularly sensitive to air pollutants because much of it is made up of exposed membrane. Lungs are anatomically structured to bring large quantities of air (on average, 400 million litres in a lifetime) into intimate contact with the blood system, to facilitate the delivery of oxygen.

Lung tissue cells can be injured directly by air pollutants such as ozone, metals and free radicals. Ozone can damage the alveoli--the individual air sacs in the lung where oxygen and carbon dioxide are exchanged. More specifically, airway tissues which are rich in bioactivation enzymes can transform organic pollutants into reactive metabolites and cause secondary lung injury. Lung tissue has an abundant blood supply that can carry toxic substances and their metabolites to distant organs. In response to toxic insult, lung cells also release a variety of potent chemical mediators that may critically affect the function of other organs such as those of the cardiovascular system. This response may also cause lung inflammation and impair lung function.

Structure and Function

The human respiratory system is dominated by our lungs, which bring fresh oxygen (O_2) into our bodies while expelling carbon dioxide (CO_2). The oxygen travels from the lungs through the bloodstream to the cells in all parts of the body. The cells use the oxygen as fuel and give off carbon dioxide as a waste gas. The waste gas is carried by the bloodstream back to the lungs to be exhaled.

The lungs accomplish this vital process-called gas exchange-using an automatic and quickly adjusting control system. This gas exchange process occurs in conjunction with the central nervous system (CNS), the circulatory system, and the musculature of the diaphragm and the chest.

The human respiratory system can be divided into the upper respiratory tract and the lower respiratory tract. The upper respiratory tract includes the following rigid structures:

- Nasal cavities: Filter the air we breathe and provide a sense of smell.
- Pharynx: Acts in the respiratory and the digestive system.
- Larynx: Link between the pharynx and the trachea. Generates the voice with the presence of vocal folds.
- Trachea: The trachea is the bond with the lower respiratory tract. This is a flexible structure allowing the air to go down to the lungs.

In addition to gas exchange, the lungs and the other parts of the respiratory system have important jobs to do related to breathing. These include:

- Bringing all air to the proper body temperature.
- Moisturizing the inhaled air for necessary humidity.
- Protecting the body from harmful substances by coughing, sneezing, filtering or swallowing them, or by alerting the body through the sense of smell.
- Defending the lungs with cilia (tiny hair-like structure), mucus and macrophages, which act to remove harmful substances deposited in the respiratory system.

Diagram of Human Respiratory System

Human Cardiovascular System

The cardiovascular system has two major components: the heart and a network of blood vessels. The cardiovascular system supplies the tissues and cells of the body with nutrients, respiratory gases, hormones, and metabolites and removes the waste products of cellular metabolism as well as foreign matter. It is also responsible for maintaining the optimal internal homeostasis of the body and the critical regulation of body temperature and pH.

The inhalation of air pollutants eventually leads to their absorption into the bloodstream and transport to the heart. A wide spectrum of chemical and biological substances may interact directly with the cardiovascular system to cause structural changes, such as degenerative necrosis and inflammatory reactions. Some pollutants may also directly cause functional alterations that affect the rhythmicity and contractility of the heart. If severe enough, functional changes may lead to lethal arrhythmias without major evidence of structural damage to the myocardium.

There also may be indirect actions secondary to changes in other organ systems, especially the central and autonomic nervous systems and selective actions of the endocrine system. Some cytokins released from other inflamed organs may also produce adverse cardiovascular effects, such as reducing the mechanical performance and metabolic efficiency of the heart and blood vessels. Many chemical substances may cause the formation of reactive oxygen.

This oxidative metabolism is considered to be critical to the preservation of cardiovascular function. For example, oxygen free radicals oxidize low-density lipoproteins, and this reaction is thought to be involved in the formation of the atherosclerotic plaques. Oxidized low-density lipoproteins can injure blood vessel cells and increase adherence and the migration of inflammatory cells to the injured area. The production of oxygen free radicals in heart tissues have been associated with arrhythmias, and heart cell death.

Heart and Lung Diseases

Heart and lung illnesses and diseases are common in Canada, and there are many factors that can increase the chances of contracting them such as smoking and genetic predisposition. The role of air pollution as the underlying cause remains unclear but is the subject of considerable research.

However, it is clear that air pollution, infections and allergies can exacerbate these conditions. An early diagnosis can lead to appropriate treatment and ensure a normal or close to normal quality of life. In many cases however, there is no cure and those affected may die prematurely. The following are the most prevalent diseases:

Minor Lung Illnesses-the common cold is the most familiar of these, with symptoms including sore throat, stuffy or runny nose, coughing and sometimes irritation of the eyes.

Lung Infections-croup, bronchitis, and pneumonia are caused by viruses or bacteria and are very common. Symptoms may include cough, fever, chills and shortness of breath.

Asthma-is an increasingly common chronic disease among children and adults. It causes shortness of breath, coughing or wheezing or whistling in the chest. Asthma attacks can be triggered by a variety of factors including exercise, infection, pollen, allergies and stress. It can also be triggered by a sensitivity to non-allergic types of pollutants present in the air such as smog.

Chronic Obstructive Pulmonary Disease (COPD)-is also known as chronic obstructive lung disease and encompasses two major disorders: emphysema and chronic bronchitis. Emphysema is a chronic disorder in which the walls and elasticity of the alveoli are damaged. Chronic bronchitis is characterized by inflammation of the cells lining the inside of bronchi, which increases the risk of infection and obstructs airflow in and out of the lung.

Smoking is responsible for approximately 80% of COPD cases while other forms of air pollution may also influence the development of these diseases. Symptoms include cough, production of mucous and shortness of breath. It is important to note that no cure exists for people suffering from COPD although healthy lifestyle and appropriate medication can help.

Lung Cancer-is the most common cause of death due to cancer in women and men. Cigarette smoke contains various carcinogens and is responsible for most cases of this often fatal disease. The symptoms of lung cancer begin silently and then progress to chronic cough, wheezing and chest pain. Air pollution has been linked somewhat weakly to lung cancer.

Coronary Artery Disease-refers to the narrowing or blocking of the arteries or blood vessels that supply blood to the heart. This disease includes angina and heart attack which share similar symptoms of pain or pressure in the chest.

Unlike angina, the symptoms caused by heart attack do not subside with rest and may cause permanent damage to the heart. Smoking, lack of exercise, excess weight, high cholesterol levels in the blood, family history and high blood pressure are some of the factors that may contribute to this disease.

Heart Failure-is a condition in which the heart is unable to cope with its work load of pumping blood to the lungs and the rest of the body. The most common cause is severe coronary artery disease. The main symptoms are shortness of breath and swelling of the ankles and feet.

Heart-Rhythm Problems-are irregular or abnormal rhythms of the heart beat. In some cases heart-rhythm problems are caused by coroneary artery disease. Symptoms of heart-rhythm problems influttering in the chest (palpitation) and feeling light-headed. Some heart-rhythm problems are life-threatening and need emergency treatment.

Pyramid of Health Effects

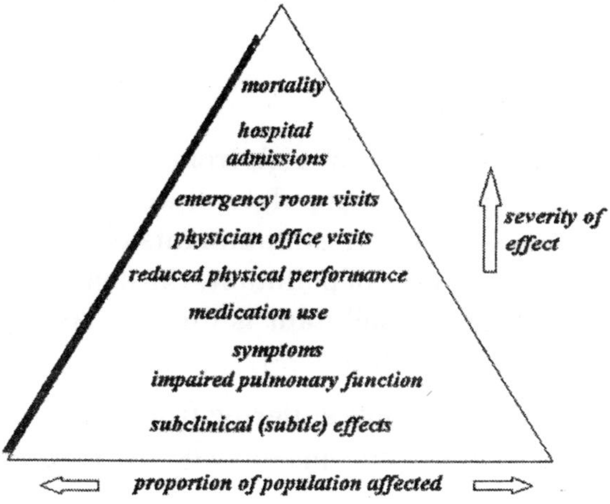

Air pollution can affect both the respiratory and cardiac systems. The health effects of air pollution can be seen as a pyramid, with the mildest but not common effects at the bottom of the pyramid, and the least common but more severe at the top of the pyramid. The pyramid demonstrates that as severity decreases the number of people affected increases.

Health Endpoints Associated with Increased Air Pollutants Levels

- Mortality: All non-accidental mortality causes
- Hospital Admissions: Cardiovascular and Respiratory Hospital Admissions
- Emergency Room Visits: Visit to an emergency department
- Asthma Symptom Days: Exacerbation of asthma symptoms in individuals with diagnosed asthma
- Restricted Activity Days: Days spent in bed, missed from work, and days when activities are partially restricted due to illness
- Acute Respiratory Symptoms: Respiratory-related symptoms such as chest discomfort, coughing and wheezing

Population at Risk

Although everyone is at risk from the health effects of air pollution, certain sub-populations are more susceptible. Individual reactions to air contaminants depend on several factors such as the type of pollutant, the degree of exposure and how much of the pollutant is present. Age and health are also important factors.

The elderly and people suffering from cardio-respiratory problems such as asthma appear to be the most susceptible groups. Children and newborns are also sensitive to the health effects of air pollution since they take in more air than adults for their body weight and consequently, a higher level of pollutants. People who exercise outdoors on hot and smoggy days are also at greater risk due to their increased exposure to pollutants in the air.

Leading Causes of Hospitalization

Respiratory and cardiovascular diseases are among the leading causes of hospitalization in Canada. In 1996-1997 there were 3.16 million hospital admissions in Canada of which cardiovascular and respiratory diseases accounted for 15% and 9%, respectively.

Air pollution exacerbates the condition of people with respiratory and cardiovascular diseases and causes measurable increases in the rates of hospitalization for these diseases. We do not yet understand the role of air pollution in causing these illnesses in the Canadian population.

Leading Causes of Death

Cardiovascular and respiratory diseases are among the leading causes of death in Canada. In 1997, 37% and 9% of over 200 000 deaths were related to cardiovascular and respiratory diseases respectively.

Air pollution causes measurable increases in non-accidental mortality.

Estimating Health Benefits

When examining a specific pollution-reduction option (such as changing gasoline composition) regulators may estimate the reduction in health effects that are expected, and the value to society of avoiding those health problems.

As a society, we pay for the health effects of air pollution in many ways. Additional health care costs for the treatment of these effects may come from any of the following: hospital admissions, visits to the emergency room or doctor's office, homecare service, medication such as inhalers for asthma. Other considerations include lost productivity in the workplace, lost wages due to sick time, out of pocket expenses incurred while ill (e.g., additional child care costs), and, finally lost quality of life or life itself.

A recent study examined the economic value of reducing the health effects of air pollution by introducing cleaner vehicles and fuels in Canada. This study found that the economic value of avoiding these health effects was $24 billion over a period of 24 years, compared to a cost of $6 billion to implement the program. This methodology has been used by Health Canada and Environment Canada in a number of initiatives to examine the benefits of control measures.

Bibliography

Becker, Randy; Henderson, J. Vernon : *Effects of air quality regulation on decisions of firms in polluting industries*, Cambridge, MA : National Bureau of Economic Research, 1997.

Bennett, Graham : *Air pollution control in the European Community : implementation of the EC directives in the twelve member states*, London; Boston : Graham & Trotman, 1991.

Bienenstock, John : *Immunology of the lung and upper respiratory tract*, New York, McGraw-Hill, 1984

Biermann, Frank : *Saving the atmosphere : international law, developing countries and air pollution*, Frankfurt am Main; New York, 1995

Boubel, Richard W.: *Fundamentals of air pollution*, San Diego, Academic Press, 1994

Brain, Joseph D : *Variations in susceptibility to inhaled pollutants : identificiation, mechanisms, and policy implications*, Baltimore, Johns Hopkins University Press, 1988

Brain, Joseph D; Proctor, Donald F.; Reid, Lynne M. : *Respiratory defense mechanisms*, New York, M. Dekker, 1977.

Bryner, Gary C. : *Blue skies, green politics : the Clean Air Act of 1990 and its implementation*, Washington, D.C., CQ Press, 1995

Chilton, Kenneth W.; Huebner, Stephen : *Has the battle against urban smog become "mission impossible?"*, St. Louis, Mo., Center for the Study of American Business, 1996.

Chretien, Jacques; Dusser, Daniel : *Environmental impact on the airways : from injury to repair*, New York, M. Dekker, 1996.

Dungworth, D. L.; Mohr, Ulrich : *Inhalation toxicology : the design and interpretation of inhalation studies and their use in risk assessment*, New York, Springer-Verlag, 1988

Farmer, David; Humphrey, John : *Safe to breathe? : the legal and practical implications of workplace exposure limits*, Horsham, West Sussex, Kingwood Pub., 1984

Friedlaender, Ann Fetter : *Approaches to controlling air pollution*, Cambridge, MIT Press, 1978.

Kay, A. B; Goetzl, Edward J. : *Current perspectives in the immunology of respiratory diseases*, New York, Churchill Livingstone, 1985.

Miller, E. Willard; Miller, Ruby M. : *Environmental hazards : air pollution : a reference handbook*, Santa Barbara, Calif., 1989.

Ozkaynak, Haluk; Spengler, John D. : *Health effects of airborne particles*, Cambridge, Harvard University, 1986.

Parkes, W. Raymond : *Occupational lung disorders*, Oxford; Butterworth-Heinemann, 1994.

Rajan, Sudhir Chella : *The enigma of automobility : democratic politics and pollution control*, Pittsburgh, University of Pittsburgh Press, 1996.

Rose, John : *Environmental health : the impact of pollutants*, New York, Gordon and Breach Science Publishers, 1990.

Samet, Jonathan M; Spengler, John D. : *Indoor air pollution : a health perspective*, Baltimore, Johns Hopkins University Press, 1991.

Tucker, William; Leaderer, B.P.; Molhave, L.; Cain, W.S. : *Sources of indoor air contaminants : characterizing emissions and health impacts*, New York, New York Academy of Sciences, 1992.

INDEX

R

S

T

U

V

□□□